For Of Such As These

A Child Becomes God's Messenger of Love

MARIE GRISSOM

WESTBOW
PRESS®
A DIVISION OF THOMAS NELSON
& ZONDERVAN

WestBow Press books may be ordered through booksellers or by contacting:

WestBow Press
A Division of Thomas Nelson & Zondervan
1663 Liberty Drive
Bloomington, IN 47403
www.westbowpress.com
1 (866) 928-1240

ISBN: 978-1-9736-6677-6 (sc)
ISBN: 978-1-9736-6678-3 (hc)
ISBN: 978-1-9736-6676-9 (e)

Library of Congress Control Number: 2019908292

Print information available on the last page.

WestBow Press rev. date: 11/01/2019

Dedication

First and foremost I dedicate this book to my Lord and Savior, Jesus Christ, who whispered the words into my spirit, monitored my ramblings, and proved his love daily.

This writing is also dedicated in loving memory of our daughter, Kimberly Dawn, whose smile still captivates us after all these years. In visions, we continue to see her run toward us with outstretched arms. We can almost touch her and feel the warmth of her loving embrace.

ACKNOWLEDGMENTS

My grateful appreciation to the following without whom this book would not be possible.

To my husband for your unfailing love, understanding, and devotion through the years.

To our wonderful parents, Buck and Leona, and Mary and J.D., who put their lives on hold in order to give us, and our children, the strength, love, and assistance we needed in a desperate time.

To our son, Dirk, who lived in the aftermath of a devastating trial and demonstrated unprecedented courage and strength. Thank you for insisting your sister's story be made public, and for holding me accountable to fulfill my promise. Thank you for blessing our family with your wife, Heather.

To our daughter Kristi, who laughed and smiled her way into our hearts and helped heal our wounds. Thank you for the love you have bestowed upon us.

To our grandchildren, Jake, Brandon, Madison, and Lee who make love easy and give us endless joy. Each of you has filled a void we never knew existed.

To my dear friends, Sandra, Faye, and Doris who pushed,

prodded, and prayed for me to complete this work. Thank you for your unending support.

Lastly, to every physician, nurse, and staff member who is a part of the medical community, I thank you for dedicating your lives to healing the sick and tenderly supporting their families.

INTRODUCTION

As a young girl, I accepted Jesus as my Savior, but until I became embroiled in the greatest battle of my life, I never understood that Jesus longed to cradle me in my times of distress, and yearned to feel at home in my heart.

I knew the story of Jesus, but I didn't know he would become the central figure in my own story. When I was pressed down beyond endurance, Jesus called me to sit with him, and to drench myself in his love.

"Lord, why is this happening? Have I done something unforgivable? Am I unlovable?"

He whispered, "I loved you enough to die in your place."

This precious moment with Jesus was the beginning of our family's three-month long journey with God. At the time, I knew nothing about the things he would reveal nor the things he would do. I had only experienced the beginning—and not the end—of our story.

Our sojourn ingrained such a profound effect upon me that years later I continued to mourn the loss of the incomparable presence of Jesus I once possessed. One day in a conversation with my brother, I confessed my desire for the close relationship I once shared with my Savior.

"Wes, I don't know what's wrong. At one time, I was so close to Jesus it seemed as though I could reach out and touch him. His presence was palpable, and nothing could separate us. But now, no matter how hard I try, or how much I pray, it's just not the same."

His eyes, welling with tears, searched mine. "Little sister, don't you know you're just homesick?"

Yes, I thought. That's it! For three long months, Jesus carried me in his arms. When I was too weak to stand, he held me upright. When I was afraid, he sheltered me. I dwelled in Jesus, and he dwelled in me. I experienced a glimpse of heaven—being at home with the Lord.

Among all the answers to prayer, and the amazing acts of kindness Jesus performed during our ninety days of oneness, he requested only one thing in return. His spirit whispered into mine, "Write these things down."

As impossible as it seemed, I knew Jesus had assigned me a task, and my soul could never find peace until I surrendered to him.

Trembling, I fell on my knees. "I don't understand it Lord, but if you can take this pebble of a woman and make something good come from the ashes of our lives, I'll follow your leading. Whatever happens in our situation, whether good or bad, I will write these things down and praise your name while giving you all the glory."

Over forty years in the making, not one day passed without me thinking of my promise. I often attempted to put it away from my thoughts, and deny my assignment, but God would not allow it. He bothered my mind and held me accountable. When my work stalled, the Holy Spirit visited me at night, and reminded me of thoughts and events I had pushed from my memory. He inscribed them upon my heart until I rose to write each word down. He spoke; I listened.

For a hurting soul, a frightened mother, someone who

hasn't met Jesus, or anyone riding the waves of despair, *For of Such as These* is meant for you. In its pages, you will discover the steadfast power of a loving God who held our family together when it was assaulted from every corner, and an indescribable peace that continuously surrounded us.

This beautiful story of God's unending love, and unlimited power, is just as relevant today as it was in 1974. Its message is simple: For whatever situation you find yourself in today, Jesus is the answer. I pray that this account of our journey will tug your spirit and hug your heart.

CHAPTER 1 - LOVE BLOOMS
WHERE GOD PLANTS

Faith does not exempt us from heartaches; instead, heartaches often increase our faith. In fact, when we are stripped of everything we hold dear, and the only thing remaining is our faith in God, faith is all we need.

In the fall of 1973, our young family knew nothing about heartaches, sickness, poverty, nor any other misfortunes in life. Married during the semester break of our junior year in college, Dan and I were now the parents of two beautiful children with another one on its way. In the chaotic world of war, protests, and bell-bottom pants, we were blessed to know exactly how each of our days would begin and end—with love.

Two-year-old Kimberly Dawn stuffed the last remnants of bacon into her mouth, wiped her hands, scrambled down from her chair, and waited expectantly for the orange and white melamine plates. Her soft blond hair stood in tousled ringlets from her night's rest, and yet, she was the sweetest sight on earth. I hurriedly gathered the dishes and placed them in her outstretched hands.

"I will take them to the sink Mom, because I'm your big helper."

While I ran water for the dishes, Kim climbed up the steps of a wooden stool positioned in front of the kitchen sink. "Mom, why does Daddy have to go to work? I miss him."

"So you can have pretty dresses, and Dirk can have new boots."

She giggled. "Mom, Daddy said I will always be his little girl."

"Yes, sweetie. That's right."

"Uh-huh, and Daddy calls me 'Sugar' too."

Repressing a chuckle, I gently tapped her nose with the tip of my finger. "That's because you're sweet as sugar."

Steadying herself on the edge of the counter, she pivoted toward me.

"You know what, Mom?"

"What, Kim?"

"I love you. And I love Daddy. And I love Dirkie. And I love Granny and Pawpaw. And I love Grandma and Grandpa. And I love Missy."

"Yes, honey, I know you do."

"And you know what, Mom?"

"What, honey?"

"You love me. And Daddy loves me. And Dirkie loves me. And Granny and Pawpaw love me. And Grandma and Grandpa love me. And Missy loves me."

I leaned down to plant a kiss upon Kim's forehead before handing her the first plate. "Yes honey, everyone loves you."

Water splashed over the sink and counter when she dunked

the plate into the rinse water, then lifted it up and immersed it once more before putting it in the rack to dry.

"Mom, does Jesus love me?"

"Of course he does. What did you learn in Bible School?"

She scrunched her eyes in contemplation, then with a burst of energy, giggled and threw her hands open wide in reply. "That Jesus loves me, and God made the trees and flowers, and he made me!"

Her joy invaded my heart. "Yes, sweetie, God certainly made you."

"Mom, did God make Dirkie too?"

"Yes, God made him too."

"Is God gonna make our baby?"

"Yes, God is making our baby right now. It won't be long before you have a new baby brother or sister."

"Mom, I'm gonna help you take care of our baby. I'm gonna *wock* it and feed it, just like I do my baby."

I pictured the poor, tattered doll she perpetually held in one hand over her heart. "You will be a wonderful big sister Kimmie."

My little helper gazed toward me. "Mom, I love our baby."

Kim's eyes sparkled with love; wet hands clasped me in a hug while she brushed a soft kiss upon my cheek. She withdrew from the kiss in silence. Her beautiful blue eyes consumed me. Like magnets, they drew me into the depths of her soul.

I held her tightly while silently praying, "Lord, I can no more understand the love I see in her eyes, than I can comprehend the unmerited love you've bestowed upon me, but I know Kimmie's heart is somehow intertwined with yours. With each kiss, I sense her pleading with me to search the recesses of her soul, and to imprint the love I find there, into my own heart and memory. Father, what is she trying to tell me?"

"I'm gonna go wake up Dirkie, Mom."

Kim gave me another kiss, and punctuated it with "I love you," before jumping down from the stool. She paused briefly to give Missy, our dachshund puppy, a hug before racing down the hall to rouse her big brother.

Screeching to a sudden halt outside his door, she tiptoed into the room, used her hands and feet as leverage to propel herself onto the bed, and rolled until she lay face to face with five-year-old Dirk. Content to lie quietly beside her brother until he was fully awake, she lay silent and still.

Rarely annoyed by his sister's morning ritual, Dirk opened one eye and sleepily murmured, "Hi, Kim."

She sprang into action. Her hands rhythmically tapped her brother on the arm while she pleaded, "Wake up Dirkie; Mom's making you *cimmamon* toast. I want to play *wis* you. I love you."

He yawned and stretched before muttering, "Okay Kim; I'll get up."

Tumbling out of bed, he sprinted down the hall with his little sister in tow. "I'll be Daniel Boone, and you be Mingo, okay?"

"Okay! I'll go get the guns! Come on Missy. Let's go!"

Dirk donned his coonskin cap and leather fringed jacket, while Kim adjusted the feathers in her headdress, then reached for her faux buckskin vest. Dirk patiently buckled a black twin holster with matching silver pistols around his sister's tiny waist before pulling his rifle out of the wooden toy box.

When the two were properly attired, they dropped to the floor, and crawled on their bellies toward a tunnel fashioned from dining room chairs and procured blankets. Dirk silently motioned for his sister to follow him as they wiggled their way through the dark tunnel. After clearing the final chair, they quickly jumped up to hide behind its structure, and trapped three imaginary bandits.

"K-Pow! Bang, Bang! P-shew, P-shew!"

The bad guys were hastily dispatched to jail, and the two frontiersmen galloped away in search of other nefarious characters.

I paused from my daily chores to watch my two offspring. I couldn't remember another time in my life when I had felt such contentment. I proudly called myself a stay-at-home mom with a degree in education. Our income bordered on meager, but despite the budget restraints, joy filled our home. I loved being a mother. Nothing could take the place of my children's absolute love and trust. It was worth the sacrifice to me. Another income couldn't replace these treasured moments.

Kim entered the world exactly one day following Dirk's third birthday. When Dirk held his little sister for the first time, he surrounded her tiny right hand in his left, and in that moment, an irrevocable bond was forged between them. Long before Kim took her first steps, the two became best friends and inseparable. They were protective of one another, and content with their world. Dirk never thought of doing anything without his little sister, and Kim was his ever loyal playmate.

"Mom! Mom! Can we go outside? Please! Please!"

Their plea, along with Kim's tugging on my skirt, brought me back from my reverie and into the present. "Yes, I think it's warm enough if you both wear jackets, but first, you two need to get dressed."

The children scattered in opposite directions. Dirk took one last bite of toast before running to get dressed, while Kim scampered toward her closet to find her favorite pink top with matching pants. Hoping my independent daughter would allow me to assist her, I followed Kim to her room.

As I secured the last buckle on her shoes, Dirk appeared beside us. "Kim, you wanna race?"

She jumped up from the floor. "Yes! I'm gonna win this time!"

"I don't know Kim; I'm a lot bigger than you."

She spun toward me. "I'm gonna run really fast Mom!"

"I know you will do your very best honey."

I bent down to give each child a hug, then walked them to the back door and held it open for them while cautioning, "Y'all have fun, and remember, don't go near the street."

The two trotted outside. Dirk took Kim's hand to help her down the steps, then both stood side by side behind the chalked line on the sidewalk.

I watched from the window as Dirk called, "Ready … Set … Go!"

Kim shrieked, and they both took off across the lawn with Missy running back and forth between the two yelping at their heels. Kimmie furiously pumped her short little legs, but regardless of how hard she tried, Dirk easily pulled ahead of her and touched the elm tree first.

Kim breathlessly protested, "Dirkie, you winned!"

In one swift movement, Dirk swung his arm over her shoulders in consolation. "It's okay Kim; I'm bigger than you."

Her sad eyes looked up toward her brother; she wrapped her arms around his waist. "I love you Dirkie."

"Come on; we'll do it again," he soothed. "This time I'll give you a head start."

The two lined up once more at the edge of the porch.

"Ready … Set … Go!"

Kim ran toward the tree while Dirk remained behind and counted, "One … Two … Three …"

A sharp pain ran across my abdomen. My hand rubbed the

rounded spot directly beneath my heart. "Little one, I think you're dancing the 'Texas Two-Step' today. You must be anxious to join in all the fun."

I smiled with pleasure. Love encircled our household. Our lives must, by necessity, soon change. Dirk was scheduled to begin kindergarten in January, and we expected our third child in mid-February. We would make new memories, and record new milestones, but these moments were firmly locked away forever in my heart.

Long before the days of laptops, cell phones, and advanced medical technology, ours was the life we dreamed of and were blessed with, until a raging storm descended upon us, and threatened to shatter our lives into a million pieces. To the world, it appeared as though tragedy struck our home with its most cruel blow, yet I am convinced it was nothing short of a marvelous plan directed by our gracious Lord and performed unwittingly by each of us. God, in his infinite wisdom, maintained control over everything that happened, and each person involved merely acted out a part already cast for him in heaven.

Jesus said, "Let the little children come to me, and do not hinder them, for the kingdom of heaven belongs to such as these" (Matt. 19:14 NIV).

Chapter 2 - Gathering Clouds

The storms of life take us to the depths of the sea, but when we attune our ears to the voice of the Almighty Father, we'll be piloted into the perfect will of God.

February, 1974

The cold winter days stretched longer than anyone anticipated. A major outbreak of one particularly tenacious virus was spreading rapidly throughout Oklahoma, and down into our area in the Texas Panhandle. With colds, stomach viruses, and tonsillitis plaguing our children, long weeks had lumbered by since everyone in our household enjoyed good health. Consequently, I wasn't alarmed when Kim slept later than usual; in fact, I hoped it signaled an end to a long siege of illness.

Summoned by the aroma of freshly brewed coffee, Dan ambled into the kitchen. His eyes scanned the room, "Where's your little helper?"

"Shhh!" I whispered. "Kim's still asleep."

"Well," he drawled. "Maybe that means she's on the mend."

"I hope so."

"Oh, she'll be okay. Dirk brings home every germ he picks

up at school, and passes it on to Kim. She's just having a tough time getting well."

He leaned his sturdy frame against the counter and took a sip of coffee before turning his full attention upon me. "I'm more worried about you. I thought for sure we were about to make a run to the hospital last night in the middle of a snow storm. Those contractions were pretty bad."

"No, just another false alarm. I could swear this baby is using my body for a boxing arena."

"The way things are going this one might be a little pistol."

"Those two little ole ladies who sit behind us at church are convinced we're having a boy. If he's anything like you, he just might be an ornery little one."

"Who? Jenney and Irene? How could they know it's a boy? Even Dr. Paul doesn't have a crystal ball to tell you that!"

"It's something about the way I'm carrying the baby. It's just an old wives' tale."

He rolled his eyes upward, and bit his bottom lip to suppress a laugh. "Blondie, when you're stretching to reach five-foot-four, how else are you gonna carry a baby?"

I shot him a look of feigned vexation. "Not everyone can be six feet tall and strong as an ox."

Ignoring my chagrin, he winked. "And no one else could be my little blond-haired woman."

Strictly a boots and jeans man, Dan was Texas born and bred. Long before he was old enough to have a license, he drove trucks, hunted with his dad, herded cattle, and rode horses across miles of ranchland. As a teenager, he worked long hours stacking bales of hay by hand. In his words, "It kept me in shape for the two things I loved, baseball and football." Dan was bold, gregarious, and the polar opposite of me.

Unable to think of a comeback, I handed him a plate of

sausage and eggs. "You better eat your breakfast before it gets cold. I'll go make sure Dirk is up and getting dressed for school."

Dan carried his plate to the table and sat down. "Babe, stay here this morning. I'll take him to school. You and Kim don't need to get out in this weather. Stay home and get some rest."

I bent down and kissed his forehead. "Thanks; I really don't want to disturb Kim if she's sleeping."

When both Dan and Dirk were fed and safely out the door, I walked down the hall to check on my little helper. She was awake, and quietly waiting for me.

"How are you feeling today, Kimmie?"

"Mommy, I don't feel good."

"Does your tummy hurt?"

"Yes, and my head hurts really bad."

I checked her temperature. The thermometer registered one hundred and one degrees. "Looks like you've caught another bug. I'm sorry honey. I'll be back in a minute."

I made an appointment with our doctor, then drove Kim to the clinic. Dr. Paul diagnosed tonsillitis for the third time, and wrote her a prescription. I could not wait for this miserable winter to be over. Please Lord; help me get these kids well!

Upon our return home, I gave Kim her medication, tucked her into bed, and sat with her until she fell into an exhausted sleep. I used her nap time to scrub the kitchen and tidy the living room. It seemed important to me at the time to keep my home in order, for aside from the recent illnesses which repeatedly afflicted the children, our lives could not be better. Our family's third child was due within a matter of days, and I wanted everything to be perfect for its arrival.

After completing my tasks, I walked down the hall to check on Kim. Her eyes were open, but she lay conspicuously still. I sat down beside her and touched her forehead; she remained feverish. I leaned backward to study her face and frail body. My internal "Mom Alarm" sounded. Something's wrong! This isn't an ordinary infection.

Kim lay motionless on the bed—as if each movement caused her severe pain. For the first time in her short life, she refused my invitation to rock her. Her familiar chatter transformed into an occasional, "No, thank you," or "Yes", when asked a question. My heart screamed, "Something terrible is happening to my child!" Yet, my mind refused to listen, and I pushed away each frightening thought.

With the help of the medication, Kim felt somewhat better within a few days, but she had no energy. An unknown agent was sapping the life from our sweet child. She sat in her wooden rocking chair for long periods of time tenderly cuddling her "baby." When she no longer possessed the strength to sit alone, she crawled up into my lap. Hugging me, she said, "Mom, please hold me."

On Friday, the fifteenth day of February, just one week after she first became ill, the virulent strain struck again. This attack descended upon Kim with an unprecedented viciousness. At three o'clock in the morning, she awoke with unrelenting nausea and vomiting. The following hours robbed her of a single moment of peace. Pain radiated from her neck, head, and eyes while she cried in my arms. "Mom-my, my head hurts so bad!"

I've never felt as inept and powerless as when she looked to me for help in those early morning hours before dawn. Dan worriedly paced while I fought to hide my fear from Kim. Thankfully, God answered my prayer to ease this latest assault on her frail system. By six in the morning, the vomiting came to an end, but the pain pounding in her eyes and head increased with intensity.

When the clinic doors opened, I carried Kim, bundled up in her coat, with a blanket covering her light-sensitive eyes, into the waiting room. I begged the receptionist, "Please, can someone check her immediately? She's been in terrible pain for hours!"

Dr. Paul had the day off, but we were ushered into a room where Kim could be seen by his associate. The doctor quickly examined her before making his diagnosis.

"I think this is just a continuation of the same infection. Keep giving her the antibiotic for the full ten days. This must simply run its course. Nothing further can be done at this point."

I spoke with urgency. "She's been sick for over a week now. I've given her the medication, but she's worse now than before. This is more than a simple headache; she can hardly move because of the pain. There must be something we can do!"

He studied the floor at length before answering. "Well, there's a new flu virus going around. I'll try a different medication just to be on the safe side."

Before leaving the room, the doctor patted me on the shoulder and said, "Both mother and daughter will feel better after a good night's rest."

I hesitated. Could my exhaustion be causing me to overreact? I placed my hands beneath Kimmie to lift her from the exam table and heard a primal moan escape her throat from the sudden movement. Pulling my thoughts from the place I had hidden them, my mind immediately recycled my worst fears. Why can't *anyone* see what I know to be true? This is much more serious than anyone suspects.

I made a quick stop at the pharmacy for the new medication

and drove home while praying, "Lord, something's wrong. Father, I don't want this! Take it from us. Please let the new prescription work."

After lunch, my mother dropped by to check on us. I noticed the concern in her eyes while she held Kim and lovingly comforted her. Kimmie's pain was so great she never spoke.

Shortly before three o'clock, Mother announced, "I'll go pick Dirk up at school. He can spend the weekend with us. He doesn't need to be exposed to this, and you have your hands full taking care of Kim." I accepted her offer with gratitude.

By late afternoon, I began to panic. No matter what the doctor believed, something inside of me kept repeating, "This is not a common virus or tonsillitis!"

The new medication was not working, and I watched my child rapidly deteriorate. An eerie sense of unease and impending calamity encompassed my being. Kim sensed something as well. On Wednesday and Thursday, she preferred to lie in bed; now she refused to move from my arms. I held her tightly while rocking her in our "special chair."

I was in the last days of a difficult pregnancy. Dr. Paul placed me on afternoon rest and restricted me from out of town travel during the last trimester. As I sat hour after hour rocking and holding my ailing child, my body screamed for relief, but my comfort mattered very little to either of us while my child and I desperately clung to one another for reassurance.

Back and forth the rocking continued. Only the creaking of the chair and my soft humming of lullabies broke the silence. Kim remained mute and lethargic while I stroked her hair and leaned down to place a kiss on her warm forehead. I reached for her hand, brought it to my lips, and inhaled the sweet scent of her favorite pink lotion.

Half an hour before Dan came home from work, I looked

down at the child lying in my arms. As I beheld her face, something so powerful and crushing came over me that I was plunged into darkness beneath its weight. The room whirled about me; I struggled to regain control and fight my way back. Whether this was only a mere thought or a premonition, the force of it made my entire body quiver and quake. My child, my beautiful, sweet Kimmie is dying! I know it with every fiber of my being!

Whatever this was surging through me, Kim experienced also. At that exact moment, she lifted herself for the first time in hours, and threw her arms around me. Together we cried, squelching screams and clinging to one another for what seemed like hours until we had quenched this innate feeling.

"Mommy! Mommy!" she sobbed. "Uh-uh-huh, I love you Mom!"

"Oh Kimmie, my sweet, sweet little girl, I love you with all my heart!" I cried in return. "I am right here honey. I've got you. I'll never let you go! Shhh! Shhh! It's okay baby; I've got you!"

She was so very weak, but miraculously, God's power engulfed Kim, and gave her the strength to pull back from our embrace. Her eyes locked with mine and drew me once more into the very depths of her soul. Love, transcending anything bound by this earth, emanated from her being. I pulled her to me and wrapped her tiny body with mine. This brief moment of heavenly strength abruptly vanished, and Kim gladly welcomed my supporting arms.

A weak, "Love you Mommy," broke our silence.

I struggled to keep the fear from my voice as I soothed, "Oh Kim, I love you so very much; you are my precious little girl. There is a special place in my heart reserved just for you. I don't know what I would ever do without you."

Her head lay nestled in the curvature of my neck; her warm

breath fanned across my heart. Tiny fingers brushed my eyes and lips while tracing the outline of my face. The clean scent of her hair wafted up, enveloping me with her essence. I pulled her nearer for kiss upon kiss, each firmly emphasized with the words, "I love you Kimmie."

Little hands softly patted my face in response. I tasted the saltiness of her tears as they mingled with mine. Once more, a miraculous strength surged through my daughter as God rained down his love upon us. The next moments were filled with such an indescribable outpouring of love that I cannot, on any level, adequately express the events, nor ever hope to experience anything comparable to this again in my lifetime.

I sensed the presence of angels surrounding us; they formed a circle of protection from the unseen threat. In the vortex of the swirling storm, my child and I tenderly touched and held one another to forever emblazon the images upon our minds and hearts. I pushed my inward screams to the back of my throat, and forced them into obedient silence. By God's grace, Kim's eyes remained closed. She never saw the anguish etched upon my face.

God's spirit brushed across my heart, urging me to speak to her. Inwardly, I railed against his exhortation. No! No! This can't be true! This is some awful nightmare; I can't live without my Kim! The portent was just too devastating and awful to contemplate, let alone accept; yet God compelled me to follow his leading.

"Kimmie, I love you; you will always be Mommy's precious little girl. Nothing can ever take you from me. You will be right here in my heart forever and ever. If you flew to the moon, I would come looking for you. I could hear your voice from far away and know it was you. You are a part of me, and I love every itty bitty bit of you, from your curly blond hair and beautiful blue eyes, to your hands that help me, down to your feet that run beside me everywhere I go. My precious little helper, I love you. I will always love you, no matter where you go or whatever you do."

The following moments are ours alone. I can no more transcribe the words than I can adequately describe the moment. I can only characterize it as an outpouring of pure, unadulterated love. Our hearts just simply broke, and from the chasm, an endless stream of love flowed. We bestowed kiss upon kiss, and exchanged one "I love you" for another while I cradled her head in my right hand next to my heart.

I caressed her tiny body while memorizing each facet of her being. A lifetime of unfathomable love was condensed into seconds and poured forth from our hearts. We locked ourselves together while we fought to hold on to the security which was rapidly slipping from our grasp.

This brief moment of time disintegrated as rapidly as it had come. Kim's frail body wilted in my arms like a spent flower. Unable to speak, she lay limp upon my shoulder. Instinctively, I wanted to pick her up and run as far and as fast as I could. I urgently needed to carry her to safety—away from the threatening cloud of darkness—but there was nowhere to run and no shelter from the storm. Three hours later our child lay in a hospital bed with the pain having increased so dramatically she could neither stand nor walk unassisted.

CHAPTER 3 - THE LOVE STORY

I paced back and forth in Kim's hospital room while attempting to calm my fears by silently repeating, "Now the doctor can determine what's wrong and give Kim the right medication."

Dan's presence provided the strength I needed. Hours earlier, he had driven home from work, opened the front door, and immediately assessed our situation. He took one look at Kim, and roared, "We need to get her to the hospital!"

Covering the distance to the phone in three steps, he called Dr. Paul at his home and rapidly explained Kim's condition. Just before hanging up the phone, he said, "Okay, thanks; we'll meet you in the emergency room in five minutes!"

I still remember the dark and gloomy night staring back at me as I looked out the window of Kim's hospital room. I searched the heavens. Could they bring me closer to God and provide an answer for all of this pain?

Sadly, the blackened skies emitted no response. Each time a nurse administered an injection, we waited for the medication to work its magic. But each dosage gave her mere moments of rest before she awoke with the same agonizing pain.

With each tiny movement Kim made, I rushed to her side. My heart longed to hear the words, "My head is better, Mommy," but instead, she gave the same crushing reply, "It still hurts."

For the remainder of the night and throughout the next day, Kim's condition remained the same. She lay lifeless upon the bed, refused any nourishment, and stirred only when the washcloth placed on her forehead needed dampening to provide a modicum of relief. When visitors appeared, she spoke briefly, and repeatedly answered them with the same words: "My head is still hurting."

Each time the nurses on duty entered the room, they routinely inquired, "Kim, can I get you anything?" Her reply never wavered, "Please help me!"

Sunday, the seventeenth day of February, arrived with no change in her status. The date marked the appointed time for our baby's arrival, and the third day of Kim's hospitalization. She lay lifeless upon the bed—refusing to eat and rarely speaking. The pain inside her head drummed relentlessly; vertigo accompanied the torment. My parents came to visit; Kim never spoke. Hour after endless hour dragged by.

By midafternoon, I grew weary from the apprehension and exhausted from the ceaseless pacing. I sat on the bed beside my daughter and began to gently wipe her eyes and forehead with a damp cloth. When the cloth stroked her cheek, Kim slowly opened her eyes, and for the first time in days, sat up in bed.

To my surprise, she began speaking in her familiar chatter. My hopes sprang alive when she asked about her brother. "Where's Dirkie? I miss him. Mom, I want to see Dirk."

"Sweetie, he wants to see you too. I promise I will take you to the lobby to see him as soon as you are feeling well enough. He misses you so much."

Kim reached upward to hug me, "Mom, I love you."

"Oh honey, I love you too, very much."

"Pretty soon Mom, I will get to see the baby. I will hold it, and take care of it for you. Mom, I love you."

My arms encircled her. "I love you too baby."

She gazed around the room and spotted the bouquet of balloons sent to her by friends.

"Mom, look at my balloons. Aren't they pretty? I wish Dirk could see them."

She wrapped her arms around my neck. "Mom, I love you."

"Kimmie, I can never get enough of your sweet hugs because I love you so much."

She pointed toward a small, white bear with a red heart attached to its chest. "I like my bear Mom. It's my Valentine bear. I want to hold it."

I held the bear out to her. Grasping it with one hand, she hugged me with the other. "Mom, I love you."

My heart flip-flopped. "Kimmie baby, I love you with all my heart."

She looked once more toward the bedside table and spied a gift bag of chocolate drops. Pointing toward the candy, she exclaimed, "Mom, I want one of those!"

Oh, now I know she is doing better! Kimmie wants chocolate!

I snatched the bag, ripped the foil wrapper from around one piece of candy, and placed it in her outstretched hand. Kim devoured the first morsel of food she had touched in three days. As she savored the sweet chocolate, my precious daughter looked up and recited what I had long ago entitled, "Kim's Love Story."

"You know what, Mom?"

"What, Kim?"

"I love you. And I love Daddy. And I love Dirkie. And I love Granny and Pawpaw. And I love Grandma and Grandpa. And I love Missy."

Unable to speak, I smiled with trembling lips.

"And you know what, Mom?"

"What, Kim?"

"You love me. And Daddy loves me. And Dirkie loves me. And Granny and Pawpaw love me. And Grandma and Grandpa love me. And Missy loves me."

Elation poured over me! Relief shot through my veins, and for one short moment, I dared believe the medication had at long last done its job. She is talking! My Kimmie has returned!

I leaned forward, intending to plant another kiss upon her forehead, but before my lips could connect with my sweet child, her countenance abruptly changed. Without warning, she began to sink backward in slow motion onto the bed. My hand reached out to support her head as she faded like a single blade of grass shriveling in the hot sun.

I watched helplessly while my child morphed into silence. Her eyes rapidly transformed into large glass marbles— staring—but not really seeing. I sat in stunned disbelief. Before I could catch one breath, Kim had once again vanished. Her essence evaporated as quickly as it had come. She lay motionless and unresponsive.

Chapter 4 - Visitors of Distinction

Within the hour, Dan entered the room and whispered, "Your dad is waiting in the lobby with Dirk. He needs to see his sister."

I nodded in silent agreement, and he bent down to tenderly cradle Kim in his strong arms. "Sugar, Dirk and Pawpaw are here. I'm going to take you to the lobby so you can see them."

Now only semi-conscious, Kim nestled her head into Dan's shoulder in reply.

I followed the two down the hall and into the hospital lobby. Dirk raced to his sister as soon as he saw us turn the corner of the white corridor. His hand immediately grasped Kim's in an attempt to regain the inexplicable bond which existed between the two. Dan carried Kim to the nearest bench and sat down.

Dirk sprawled across Dan's knee to gain better access to his sister. "Kim, I hope you get better soon. I miss you. Don't worry about Missy," he assured. "I'm taking real good care of her."

Dirk's hand remained in constant motion, soothing and stroking her hand. Kim valiantly tried to force open her eyes, but there were only brief flashes of the sparkling blue orbs lying beneath her long lashes. In ways understood only by them, our two children communicated in spite of the obstacles, and he received comfort from the touch of her hand.

Dan looked toward me before addressing Dirk. "Son, we need to get Kim back to bed now."

I glanced to my right and noticed my dad. Not wishing to intrude upon the moment, he stood quietly to the side observing the drama unfold while he battled unshed tears. I watched his trembling lips whisper the same words of prayer I had heard every single day of my childhood, "Most Gracious Heavenly Father; Blessed Heavenly Father ..."

Dirk stretched out his hand one last time toward his sister. He gently patted her tummy as he consoled, "Kim, you're gonna be okay. I love you."

Amid the deafening silence, she whispered a reply, "Love you Dirkie."

I remained in the lobby while Dan carried Kim back to her room. Dirk stood watching the two until they disappeared from his sight. When he turned back toward me, the air of confidence he portrayed for Kim had vanished, and I saw only fear and torment in his eyes. I pulled him into my arms for a fierce hug while wishing I could shield him from the trauma encompassing our lives.

"Dirk, Kim will get better. She is very tired, and the doctor gave her medicine to help her sleep. That's why she couldn't open her eyes and talk to you."

Sensing the seriousness of Kim's illness, he stood mute. His eyes stared into mine. I sought words to comfort him. "Honey, she heard everything you said, and I know you made her feel better. She's been asking to see you, so I am very glad you and Bob came."

I prayed these few words would be enough to alleviate his hurt and confusion. They were as close to the truth as I could manage.

Dad regained his composure enough to intervene. "Well,

big boy, while Kim is asleep, let's go see if Granny has any ice cream."

Reluctant to leave, Dirk looked toward me. I gently hugged my son once more. "It will be okay honey. Daddy and I will stay with Kim. She knows you love her."

I watched my father and son walk in lock-step toward the parking lot; my heart filled with gratitude. Mother and Dad were an integral part of our children's lives. Several times each week, Mother dropped by and invited the children to visit their "most favorite place." My parents' auto parts business contained more thrills than any theme park in the world. Mother carved out a special area in the storefront for the children and filled it with toys and art supplies, but these were often neglected in favor of the antiquated cash register and adding machine equipped with large keys and pull-down handles.

After greeting their beloved grandfather, Dirk and Kim zeroed in on the soft drink machine. Dad never failed to have the exact amount of change for each child just waiting in his pockets. With their preferred drinks in hand, they ran to the glass candy counter with its enormous assortment of snacks and candy bars.

Knowing their choices rarely wavered, Mother waited patiently to assist the children with their selections. Dirk stretched his lean torso to reach inside a canister containing packets of peanuts. With one stroke, he ripped off the seal from one of the packets, and poured the peanuts into his bottle of cola, while Kim went directly to her favorite bar of chocolate.

Dirk inevitably settled himself on one of the tall, metal stools at the service counter to sit beside Dad, whom he had dubbed, *"Bob,"* as a toddler. Kim preferred to ensconce herself in Granny's lap to devour her chocolate.

Over the course of their visit, the store's long, narrow

aisles ... housing metal bins filled with nuts, bolts and assorted parts ... became their playground. The children had complete access to every shiny tool and machine available, as well as the full attention of their doting Pawpaw and Granny. Our children adored my parents. If we must go through this valley, Mother and Dad were the best support team possible.

I turned and walked down the corridor toward Kim's room with a sense of dread. Everyone treaded on edge waiting for any sign of improvement in Kim, or at the very least, confirmation of a diagnosis and the appropriate remedy.

Mother timed her second visit of the day to coincide with the hour we expected Dr. Paul's arrival for evening rounds. Dan engaged in the same vigil by pacing up and down the corridors of the hospital. He aimed to meet privately with the doctor to get straight answers—not the softened versions Dr. Paul gave me.

Dan's frustration neared the boiling point. He saw himself as the protector of his little girl. Unfortunately, his ability to hold back this raging tidal wave equaled mine. We both lacked the power to stave the turbulent waters. Yet, he stubbornly refused to let this situation go on indefinitely.

Mother stood sentinel beside Kim when the doctor walked through the door flanked by Dan. I noted the concern, mixed with determination, etched upon my husband's face just before the doctor asked me to sit down.

"I have a proposition for you. I know you are worried about Kim, but it's my job to take care of both of you. You've been here at the hospital since Friday, so you've had at least two nights without any sleep. You need to get some rest."

I opened my mouth in protest, but Dr. Paul cut me off. "This little girl is going to be fine. We have good nurses here to take care of her, but I don't want any complications or an emergency on my hands when you go into labor."

He looked toward my mother, "Let your mom stay here with Kim tonight. You go home and get some rest. If she isn't better by tomorrow morning, I'll call a specialist."

I glanced to my right. Mother nodded her head in agreement. I trusted my mother implicitly, but I didn't want to leave. What if something happened overnight? Mom read my mind and answered, "I'll call you if anything changes."

I was outnumbered. It occurred to me Mother's timing might be part of an organized effort by my family to force me to rest. I slowly shuffled to the bed and bent down to kiss my beautiful child. Dan put his arm around me, and ushered me toward the door before I could protest any further. Stubbornly, I turned one last time toward Mother and Dr. Paul.

"She'll be fine; it's just a bad sinus infection," urged the doctor. "I'm going to increase her pain medication and try a different antibiotic. I think you will see real improvement tomorrow morning."

Mother instantly appeared at my side. This diminutive woman, the eldest of seven brothers and sisters, grew up working in the cotton fields of Texas chopping weeds and picking cotton by hand. She was no stranger to hardships, and not prone toward outward displays of affection, but her love ran deep for her family. She pulled her shoulders back to stand ram-rod straight while warding off any protest. "I'll take care of her. You need to rest."

Dan and I stopped by my parent's house to fetch Dirk before driving home. I wanted our son to spend the night with us. He was frightened, upset and confused. "But Mom, what's wrong with Kim?"

I couldn't pull many words of comfort from my depleted

reservoir, so instead, I chose to simply hold him in my arms and try to hug away the fear. "Don't worry honey; Granny is going to stay with her all night, and God is always with her. She is in good hands."

I lay beside Dirk, whisperings words of encouragement until he fell asleep, and then stepped quietly down the hall to our bed. I tossed and turned—fitfully worrying, and praying all at the same time. "Please, please, dear God, heal Kim; I love her so much!"

I glanced at the clock for the hundredth time. Would the morning ever come? My eyes began to close in weary sleep when I heard a knock on the door. I jumped up from the bed in alarm. No one would be knocking at one o'clock in the morning unless something terrible had happened!

Not taking time to find my robe, I bolted to the door with my heart pounding. I flipped on the porch light while simultaneously swinging open the door. My shoulders slumped in surprised relief; Dan's parents, Mary and J.D., stood at the threshold. Before I could utter one word, their arms engulfed me, and the tears I held at bay gushed in streams from the depths of my soul.

Dan sleepily muttered from the hallway, "What are you two doing here in the middle of the night?"

Mary went to her son, wrapped him in an embrace, and asked, "Where do you think we should be? We came to see Kim, and to help you."

After phoning earlier to check on Kim, and hearing her condition had not changed, they immediately took emergency work leaves, packed, and drove the one hundred and twenty miles to our home. Their actions did not surprise me.

Our little girl had a way of bringing out great love and affection from everyone to whom she allowed closeness. I am not speaking of perfection; Kim could get angry, become stubborn, and cry just like any child approaching three years of age. Yet no one seemed able to become upset with her, and I was no exception. No matter what she did, I could never bring myself to become angry with her. One look into those huge blue eyes could melt any heart. All four of her grandparents fell prey to those same alluring eyes and sweet smile.

At the time, Kim held the unique position of being the only little girl of five grandchildren in Dan's family. J.D., was a large, burly man, but just one hug and a simple, "I love you Grandpa," melted his stern exterior and revealed a tender heart. His brusque voice changed instantly into a soft musical lilt when speaking with her.

J.D. learned early on about Kim's love for chocolate; thus he made it his priority to have this particular treat on hand for every visit. He discovered her secret on a family fishing trip. When we were packing up the fishing gear and supplies to leave, Kim crawled up onto the seat of her grandparents' truck to ride with them.

J.D. retrieved a bag of chocolate candy from the cooler for a snack on the trip home. He first gave Dirk some of the sweet morsels and then turned to offer one to Kim. Instead of her reaching to take the proffered candy, she simply stood with her hands behind her back while eying the bag of candy.

The two stood at a stalemate until J.D. lowered his hand with the one chocolate and offered the entire bag to his granddaughter. She immediately reached for the candy, and with an enchanting smile said, "Thank you, Grandpa."

J.D. managed to choke back his laughter with a stifled chortle while smiling indulgently at his precocious granddaughter.

Mary loved each of her grandsons, but she delighted in having a little girl in the family to clothe in frilly dresses and petticoats. Each time we visited, a new dress with tons of lace and layers of petticoats awaited Kim's arrival. After welcoming us, Mary pulled the beautiful treasure from its bag and excitedly remarked, "I saw this dress, and I just knew I had to get it for Kim."

J.D. made an extra effort to have a special gift on hand for Dirk as well. Simply put, they loved their grandchildren. It seemed only natural for them to drop everything to be with Kim.

The four of us sat talking into the early hours of the morning attempting to sort the recent events while filling our conversations with empty reassurances. Shortly before three o'clock, we crawled into bed to get a few hours of rest.

Mary and I rose before dawn so we could get to the hospital as soon as possible. Darkness blanketed the sky when we walked into Kim's room. I pinned my hope on the new medication bringing about a change in Kim's condition overnight, but when I saw her lying motionless upon the bed, my heart sank. Nothing had changed.

I crept to her bed and spoke softly to her. Kim's eyes opened in a thin line when I mentioned the arrival of her other grandparents; she spoke the same bitter words, "My head is still hurting."

One look at my mother instantly told me everything I needed to know. Her face was drawn and etched with worry. She whispered, "The new medicine hasn't helped."

The morning moved tediously forward while the panic grew layer by layer. As I helplessly watched Kim endure such pain and torment, I frequently fled from her room and wept in the hallway. I alternated between praying in silence, and crying aloud to God. Couldn't He hear me? Couldn't He see the agony visiting my child?

By two o'clock in the afternoon, Dan sat across the desk from Dr. Paul in the nurses' station. A neurosurgeon in a neighboring city waited to examine Kim and run any necessary tests. My parents, along with Mary and J.D., were in Kim's room when Dr. Paul and Dan pushed through the door to relay this same information to us.

I attempted to absorb everything they spoke, but my mind locked itself solidly around the word, "neurosurgeon," and nothing else penetrated my senses. Dr. Paul spoke to us about referring her to a specialist. I don't know what I had been expecting ... or more appropriately ... avoiding, but the mere mention of a neurosurgeon caused me to tremble in fear. This couldn't be happening. This doesn't happen to people like us!

A sense of urgency permeated the room. The neurosurgeon expedited the arrangements to admit Kim into one of the area's largest hospitals. She might be there for days; we had to get packed. I pulled my thoughts back to the present, and joined Mother and Mary in gathering up all of Kim's belongings. As I picked up a vase of flowers, Dan placed his hand upon my shoulder. I turned my attention toward him. "What now?" I wondered.

CHAPTER 5 - YOU MUST STAY

Dan's eyes locked with mine. He bit his lower lip before speaking. "Babe … Dr. Paul doesn't think you should go with us. The baby could come at any time. You need to be here, not seventy-five miles away."

"I don't care! I'm going wherever Kim goes!"

The doctor voiced his concerns. "You're physically exhausted. You haven't had any rest in days. Remember, I haven't allowed you to travel for months. It's just too dangerous for you and the baby."

Weighing in with their opinions, the other family members followed Dr. Paul's lead. Mary and J.D. volunteered to drive Dan and Kim to the hospital in their car. Mary promised, "I'll be with her every minute. I'll take good care of her."

I couldn't ask for a more wonderful second mother. I never doubted Mary's ability to take excellent care of Kim. In fact, her presence gave me great comfort. The overriding problem centered on my being forced to stay behind. *I am her mother!* I am the one who is supposed to take care of her! She needs me!

"Dan, I *need* to go with you! I can't stay here when my child is in a hospital miles away. Don't ask me to do that!"

Dr. Paul interrupted, "They need to get Kim to the hospital as soon as possible. If something happens to you on the way, you'll only be delaying her treatment while endangering yourself and the baby you're carrying. Kim will be in good hands; she'll receive excellent care. You need to take care of yourself and your other two children."

I scanned the room. Tears dripped from every eye. I saw the heartbreak etched upon the faces of my husband and parents. I needed to pull myself together and do the right things for Dirk, Kim, and the baby.

I quickly bundled Kim in a blanket for the drive. Swallowing the huge lump in my throat, I addressed her with a trembling voice. "Kimmie, Daddy and Grandpa and Grandma are going to take you for a ride. Someone who can make you feel better is waiting to see you. Mommy can't go with you right now, but Grandma will take good care of you. I promise I will see you very soon baby."

She made no protest. The pain robbed her of the ability to speak or move.

I walked out of the hospital battling tears, and slipped into the back seat of Mary and J.D.'s automobile while Dan followed in our car. My arms tightly clasped Kim for the short ride to our home. Dan hurriedly packed a bag while I sat in the car clinging to my child. No more than five minutes passed before he opened the door and held it for me to exit.

I couldn't make myself get out of the car. A neurosurgeon waited in another city to admit Kim for testing, but I could not let her go. She was fearful of doctors. How could I send my child to a stranger in an unfamiliar place without accompanying her?

I held her tightly, "Kimmie, I love you! I love you baby!"

Dan leaned into the car, pried my hands from around my child, and gently placed Kim in Mary's outstretched arms. He pivoted, quickly pulled me from the car, and walked me to the front door of our home.

I thought I would shatter into a million pieces, but I could no longer beg my husband to let me go with him. I was not the only one in pain. Dan's internal struggles were depicted in the recessed furrows etched across his brow and in the pools of unshed tears welling at the corners of his eyes.

Gripping me in his arms he vowed, "Babe, I won't let anything happen to Kimmie. You've got to be strong, and take care of yourself and Dirk. I love you."

My heart had just been ripped from me in the car. My throat constricted, denying me the ability to voice a reply; I nodded my head in agreement.

"I'll call as soon as possible. Pack up and go to your Mom and Dad's house. I don't want you and Dirk here alone if you go into labor."

Silently signaling I had heard his instructions, I touched his cheek.

He hugged me fiercely before running to the car. I watched the vehicle speed down the street and make a right turn at the corner before it disappeared from my sight; trees and homes blocked any further viewing. Helplessness, coupled with a crushing fear, beset me.

I turned, opened the front door, and stepped into our dark, empty home. I stood on the precipice of a loud scream and total collapse when I heard a tapping on the door. Our next-door-neighbor watched Dan and his parents drive away with Kim. Sensing my devastation, she dashed over to check on me. By God's grace, I held back the flood of emotions riveting through me long enough to express my appreciation for her concern.

Without going into great detail, I explained our current situation. Martha proffered a hug, "I'll be praying for you. Can I help you pack?"

"Thank you," I answered, "but I just need to pack a few

things. Mother always has clothes and toys on hand for the kids. I'll be fine."

"Well, I'll go so you can pack, but call me if you need anything."

At the very second the door closed behind her, the volcano building inside of me erupted with full force. I ran to Kim's bed and splayed myself across its coverings to inhale the lingering scent of my sweet child. Clutching the corner of the coverlet, I sank to the floor and pressed my head against the bed while sobbing bitter tears.

"No Lord! You can't let this happen!"

Silent screams spewed from my throat; my body shook in agony. When at last my screams found their voice, guttural moans and high pitched shrieks echoed throughout the room. Primal cries from a heart torn asunder accompanied a watershed of tears.

"God! Dear God!" I cried. "Please; please don't take her!"

At the mention of his name, I felt my heavenly Father's arms surround me. My body rocked back and forth. I cried while God's presence cradled me like a child. I groaned, unable to express the overwhelming heartache consuming my soul.

An urgent plea erupted from the depths of my soul, "Oh Lord, take care of Kim for me. Please, please Father, protect her with your mighty hands! Hold her in your arms and love her in my place. Please God, please heal her and bring her back to me. I love her so much!"

Sorrow induces agony and shows no mercy. One can never deny it, circumvent it, or push the pause button. I could not have survived this ordeal without my Father's strength. The rocking of my body did not cease until I was spent and devoid of all emotion.

The tears dried, and from somewhere within my being, I heard the words, "It's okay child; I'm here."

By the hand of God, calm prevailed. My mind could not comprehend, nor my lips express the enormity of the situation, yet my Lord and Savior heard my inept plea for mercy. He understood the pain surging in my heart. His loving compassion surrounded me. Jesus became my ultimate sustainer and the source of my strength.

Willing my mind and body to keep busy, I pulled myself from the floor and spent the remainder of the afternoon furiously cleaning our home while trying with all my might to scrub away the torment from my heart. Two hours later, my home sparkled, and our things were packed. I drove the few blocks to my parents' home to join my son and wait for any news.

CHAPTER 6 - THE INTERMINABLE WAIT

Dan phoned shortly before seven o'clock. I heard the fear in his voice and sensed his anxiety. "The doctor thinks Kim could have meningitis. He wants to run a test tomorrow to find out for sure."

"Meningitis! How in the world did—"

"I don't know. That's just what he's thinking. But ... we did find out one thing ... Kimmie is seeing double. That's why she's so dizzy."

"Why? What's causing her to see double?"

"Nobody knows. Doc told me a lot of things can cause it."

"Please give Kim a hug for me, and tell her I love her!"

"Babe, she knows, but I'll tell her again. Try not to worry. You get some rest, and tell Dirk I love him. I'll call you tomorrow. I love you."

With tears choking my voice, I squeaked out a weak goodbye. "Love you too."

Time became my enemy. The minutes moved tortuously by while my life stood on hold. I must wait for the results of tests before Kim could be treated. I waited for the birth of my baby. Worst of all, I anxiously waited to see Kimmie. I rarely took a step without her walking beside me. She accompanied me on every shopping trip and each visit I made. How could I sit at home and wait while she was lying in a hospital without me?

I volunteered to help Mother prepare dinner, but even this small task became unbearable. I missed my little helper. With each meal preparation, Kim's feet scooted across the floor keeping pace with mine as we walked back and forth from the cupboards to the table. Her absence screamed at me with every step. An indescribable sadness descended upon me. The hours inched by.

Mere days before, our nights rang out with laughter and the noises of happy children. Dirk and Kim took turns running across the room to pounce on their daddy who lay sprawled on the couch recuperating from his long day at work. They squealed with glee when Dan bellowed like Bigfoot, grabbed one of his attackers, and held him or her at his side.

As a finale to the evening festivities, Dirk pulled his guitar from its resting place and entertained us with song after song while Kim danced to his music. We applauded as the children appropriately bowed. After bathing, the two jumped on the beds and once again engaged in playful wrestling with Dan. Quiet time followed when I read their favorite books. Our nights ended with the children's sweet bedtime prayers.

Tonight, neither joy nor the sound of children's laughter rang out. My parents and I could neither speak our thoughts nor concentrate on anything other than Kim. Staring mindlessly at the television, we sat in deafening silence. Dirk sat on the floor quietly playing with his trucks.

My mind ordered, "Do not pace. Keep still. Do not let your son see your anxiety."

After taking an eternity, bedtime at last arrived. Giving Dirk an extra hug, I tucked him into bed for the night. "I love you. Sweet dreams honey."

"Mom! I want to pray!"

Generally, Dirk needed a reminder to end his day with

prayer, but on this night our son had something important to ask God. The light from a bedside lamp cast a soft shadow across his face. When he began to pray, I gasped for air.

"Please God, make Kimmie well; we don't want her to die!"

These were the chilling words both Dan and I were too afraid to utter. Yet, they were at last spoken by a brave five-year-old child.

At half past five on Tuesday morning I slipped from the bed and walked aimlessly around my parent's home. The same thoughts drummed incessantly with each step: Kimmie's not here to say, "G'morning Mom, I love you."

I can't lift her in my arms for our G'morning hug and kiss.

My jittery heart thumped against my chest when I stepped into the dark kitchen. This isn't *my* home! It's not *my* kitchen!

Nothing is the same as it was mere days ago. I can't place Kim on the counter and watch her pull each biscuit from the package, then squish and push it into the baking pan. I won't see the imprint of her tiny fingers on the bread when I place it in the oven. I won't hear her inquire, "Mom, I'm your big helper, aren't I?"

Dan was missing from my life as well, but at least he was with Kimmie. She loved her Daddy. I closed my eyes to replay the scene I witnessed each morning between my husband and daughter:

Dan strolled into the kitchen and called out to Kimmie, "Hey, hey, hey, whatcha doing Sugar?"

"Daddy!" Kim squealed, then ran toward the outstretched

arms of the one she adored. He lifted her into the air and planted a kiss on her cheek.

"Daddy, I put the biscuits in the pan for Mom. I bringed your plate to the table Daddy. You have red jelly. I'm Mom's big helper Daddy."

"Yes Sugar, and you will always be Daddy's little girl."

Kim bobbed her head up and down in affirmation. Her hands softly patted his face. "Yes Daddy, I am your little girl, and I love Mom, and I love Dirkie, and I love you, Daddy."

I forced myself to pull away from the haunting memories. My other child needed me just as much as Kimmie. Dirk's passionate bedtime prayer spoke volumes about his understanding of Kim's situation. I decided to visit with both his teacher and the principal to apprise them of our situation.

The day trickled by with several calls from Dan, but he had nothing new to report. Doctors were still performing tests, and none of the ones completed thus far were conclusive. For each question I directed toward him, he replied, "She's about the same."

The neurologist withdrew all medication from Kim upon her arrival. Any type of medication might mask the critical neurological indicators which could lead to a diagnosis. I paced aimlessly throughout the day while dwelling upon the level of pain she must be enduring. Her suffering neared the unbearable under heavy medication. I couldn't imagine what it must be like for her now.

Wednesday morning I awoke determined to see Kim. I waited until Dirk was off to school before broaching the subject. Mother sat in a gold wingback chair in the living room. I sat down on the couch facing her.

"Mother, I need to see Kim today. I can't stand this waiting.

I need to hold her—even if it's only for a few minutes. I know I can't drive by myself. Would you please go with me?"

Exhibiting a nervous habit she inherited from her mother, Mom ran her thumb down the length of her arm, and looked out the door in contemplation. Knowing my request placed Mother in an untenable position, I waited for her to speak.

"Rea, I don't think I can do it. If something happens to you, your three kids might not have a mother. Let me call your Daddy and see if he has time to go to the hospital today. He can check on Kim, and if she's worse, then we'll think about driving you there."

I didn't like her solution, but it seemed like the only thing I could do at this point. When Mother referred to me by my childhood nick-name, I knew her heart was as sore as mine. I couldn't press her further. My sweet dad was on his way to the hospital within twenty minutes of our conversation.

Wishing I could do something other than worry and wait, I paced aimlessly throughout the house. The Holy Spirit brushed across my heart to remind me of my role. "You are never alone nor helpless. Your job is to intercede on Kim's behalf through prayer."

Immediately, I called a friend and asked her to help me set up a prayer meeting for Kim at two o'clock. Without hesitation, Joyce called every woman in the church. I was astounded when I walked into the sanctuary and saw so many friends and acquaintances gathered to pray for our little girl. These women of God were mighty prayer warriors. I knew their prayers would continue until we brought our daughter safely home.

After leaving the church, I drove to the clinic for my weekly check-up. Toward the end of my appointment, I begged, "Dr. Paul, please give me permission to travel! I need to take care of Kim! I can't stand this. I need to see her. I'll be careful; just let me go!"

He studied the air before answering me. "I think it will be a few more days before the baby arrives. I'm going to let you travel tomorrow on one condition. I want you to get plenty of rest tonight. That means you go straight home, and don't *do* anything!"

Relief flooded my soul. I thanked Dr. Paul profusely before leaving his office. I couldn't wait for Dan to call so I could tell him the wonderful news.

I drove to my parents' home, and stood sentinel at the front window to await Dad's return from the hospital. Just as I caught a flash of his yellow truck coming down the street, the phone rang. For the first time in days, I didn't run to the phone; I wanted to hear Dad's report on Kim's condition.

Mother spoke from the hallway, "Rea, it's Dan. He needs to talk to you."

I spun away from the window, charged toward the hallway, and grabbed the phone.

"Dan, is everything okay?"

"Hi, how are you feeling?"

With relief, I answered, "I'm fine. I have great news. Dr. Paul said I could travel tomorrow to visit Kim."

"Yeah, I know…"

"What do you mean? How could you know? Dr. Paul just told me half an hour ago!"

"You told me you were going to the doctor for your checkup this afternoon, so I called him before your appointment. I needed to know exactly how you were doing."

Fright ran up my spine. "Why? What's wrong?"

He took a faltering breath and exhaled before speaking. "I needed to know whether you could travel. We might have a pretty serious situation here. I want to keep you and the baby

safe … but … I think this deal with Kim overrides everything else."

"Dan, tell me what's wrong!"

"Dr. Carlton got the results back from Kim's tests today. He thinks either meningitis or some other kind of virus is causing her to develop too much cerebral fluid. The extra fluid is building up pressure in her brain, and that's probably what's causing her headaches."

Dan fell mute. I heard his labored breathing into the phone's mouthpiece. His lengthy silence stretched across the miles; terror traveled through the phone lines and pulled me into its clutches.

"Honey," I begged. "What's wrong? You have to tell me!"

"Babe … he's also looking for a tumor."

A chill ran across my shoulders. I gulped back a scream and focused instead on the bulk of information Dan disseminated.

"The doctor's scheduled X-rays and air studies for tomorrow to rule out a tumor. I don't really know what these air studies are, but it's the best way they have to see what's going on in the brain. If the tests don't show any signs of a tumor, then he'll take Kim to surgery to put in a ventricular shunt."

"What in the world is a shunt?"

"It's some kind of tube they'll put in her brain, then thread it down through a vein in her neck, and into her stomach. It's supposed to help drain the fluid and relieve the pressure in her brain."

Pneumoencephalography, commonly called an air study, was a dangerous and, as we were to later discover, very painful procedure. Dan understood I needed to be with Kim at such a crucial time, but he agonized over the decision because of the possible danger to me and the baby. In the end, he had no choice but to tell me the truth.

Chapter 7 - Uncommon Peace

Thursday, February 21

Throughout the long night, I struggled with the forces bent upon destroying our family. Surgery Lord? Brain surgery? No, this can't be happening! Too many things can go wrong when you open up the skull and touch the brain. No Lord! No! No!

Thoughts and images swirled around in my head. My child would undergo brain surgery; worse yet, doctors suspected a tumor. I couldn't cope with either reality. I lay in bed, forcing myself to give my body rest while my heart pounded and my mind raced over every conceivable danger and outcome.

"Father, I need your strength. If I say 'I trust you,' then I must believe you will take care of everything. Lord, I can't face all the dangers coming at me. You know how weak I am. Please take care of Kimmie; bring her safely through all of this. Wrap your arms around her and protect her. Hold the surgeon's hands steady. Don't let anything happen to her!"

My entreaty persisted throughout the night, and by the breaking of dawn, peace girded me. An absolute certainly of God's presence was firmly planted in my heart. The Holy Spirit swept over me, and replaced each uncertainty with total trust and assurance in God's omnipotent power.

His spirit whispered to me, "Everything is all right."

He took me to a place of perfect peace; no other words can describe the calm assurance resting in my soul.

On the way to the hospital, I remained calm. I was certain Kim would come through the tests and surgery without incident. Never before in my life had I displayed even a hint of courage when doctors and tests were involved. I delayed scheduling each immunization the children needed until the last minute simply because I could not bear to see them hurt. Once when Kim needed to have blood drawn, a second nurse held her while I stood on the opposite side of the room crying. Yet God's grace is all sustaining, and on this day, his strength kept me composed and calm in the middle of a raging storm.

My family and I arrived early. Kim's X-rays were scheduled to begin at ten o'clock, and I wanted to spend as much time with her as possible. Dan tried to prepare me for the sight I would encounter, but nothing short of the grace of God kept me from disintegrating the moment I stepped inside her small room in the Intensive Care Unit.

Kim lay in a sea of white and lost in a maze of tubes, tape, and bottles. She had been catheterized in preparation for the surgery; additionally, intravenous tubes trailed from both her left hand and foot. Small, one-inch cuts, made to inject dye into her arteries for a series of arteriograms, lined her arms and legs. Her hair lay matted upon her head with a thick, white paste used to perform three separate electroencephalograms to detect any neurological abnormalities.

Any other time I would have run screaming from the room, but at this particular moment my eyes locked solely upon the vision of two outstretched arms and Kim's quivering lips sobbing the words, *"Mommy! Mommy!"*

I wanted to sweep her up into my arms and hold her, but the

enormous amount of apparatus made it impossible. I placed my arms around her, avoiding the tangle of tubing, and kissed her gently. Self-loathing washed over me. I sat at home, wrapped up in my own self-pity, while my child endured unimaginable suffering. Not one part of her precious body had been spared throughout these procedures.

"Dear God," I silently prayed. "Don't let me cry. Help me, Lord; help me!"

Tears rolled from Kim's eyes when she exclaimed, "Mom, I missed you so much!"

I choked back tears. "Oh Kimmie, I've missed you too. Daddy and Pawpaw told me you've been a very brave little girl. I am so proud of you baby. You are Mommy's big girl, and I love you so much. I couldn't wait to get here today to see you."

In spite of her pain, Kim spoke incessantly. "I missed you too Mom, and I miss Dirkie. Why can't I see him? Mom, I love you."

Her bed overflowed with stuffed animals and hand puppets she had received from family and friends. Kim introduced me to each one before retrieving a tiny velvet dachshund lying at her side.

She bestowed a kiss upon its ear before declaring, "Mom, this is my Missy Dog. It's my favorite. It looks just like my puppy at home. Uncle Gary and Aunt Beth gave it to me. I love my Missy Dog!"

Not one drop of water, nor one morsel of food, had touched Kim's lips since her arrival at the hospital. The doctor's order prohibited anything by mouth until he completed each of the required diagnostic tests. Coupled with the previous days without sustenance at home, this marked the beginning of her seventh day without any nourishment other than the intravenous fluids being pumped through her body. She was so very thirsty, and often her mind wandered to things both cool and refreshing.

"Mom," she whispered. "I want a red ice pop and some green sherbet."

I could only make a lame promise. "Kimmie, the nurses will bring you something to drink as soon as the doctor finds out what is making your head hurt."

My words satisfied her briefly, but then she began to reflect once more upon ice cream and a cola. "Mom, can Pawpaw bring me something to drink like he does at the store?"

I pushed back a sob before softly murmuring, "Honey, when you are better, you can have anything you want. I promise sweetie!"

Her lips were dry and cracked. Her throat and mouth were parched. She licked her burning lips. "Mommy, I'm thirsty!"

I reached for a damp washcloth to soothe her burning tongue and lips while silently raging. Why must Kimmie endure such things? I can't give her the cooling liquids she craves nor do anything to relieve her suffering! Why is this happening Lord?

The hospital's Intensive Care Unit imposed strict visitation rules. Patients were allowed one brief visit every two hours. God's hand must have been upon the nurses, because I stayed with Kim, never leaving her side, for over two hours. Nurses kept their constant vigil, but each worked competently and swiftly, then retreated so my daughter and I could share these precious moments.

We used the time to hug and kiss, to dream about our coming plans when she felt better, and to simply touch one another. I held her right hand in mine—afraid to let it go. Other family members came in for brief visits, but through God's benevolence, I did not budge from Kim's side.

Shortly before ten o'clock, a tall, thin man breezed into

the room exuding an air of confidence. He leaned over the bed to examine Kim. I studied the man whom I presumed would make life or death decisions for our child. The doctor appeared surprisingly youthful, with ruddy cheeks and dark, thick hair. His slender hand flashed a light in each of Kim's eyes, but the man did not utter one word until he completed his exam.

Pushing the penlight into his coat pocket, the doctor at last acknowledged my presence. He glanced down at my protruding midsection and inquired, "Are you the mother?"

"Y...Yes," I stammered.

"Good, you're finally here. I'm Dr. Carlton; I'll be performing the surgery on your daughter. I need you to provide some missing information."

Before I could open my mouth to reply, Dr. Carlton snapped Kim's medical file open and fired one question after another at me until his forms were complete. Then, looking up from the file, he dispassionately described the scheduled procedures for the day.

Just as I began to think this doctor lacked any traits of human emotion, he gently added, "We are going to do everything we can for her."

I swallowed the lump in my throat before answering, "Thank you."

I didn't trust myself to say anything further. Kim might sense my anxiety. I wanted to beg, "Please, please take care of her! I love her more than anything in this world. Please don't let anything happen to her!"

I returned to Kim's bedside, and my sweet child began a familiar story.

"You know what, Mom?"

"What, Honey?"

"I love you. And I love Daddy. And I love Dirkie. And

I love our baby. And I love Granny and Pawpaw. And I love Grandma and Grandpa. And I love Missy."

"Yes, Kimmie. You love everyone."

"And you know what, Mom"

"What, Kimmie?"

"You love me. And Daddy loves me. And Dirkie loves me. And Granny and Pawpaw love me. And Grandma and Grandpa love me. And Missy loves me."

I never grew tired of hearing those beautiful words. Not one day ever passed without her listing each of the people she loved, and those who loved her in return. Surely this was a child capable of giving more love than any of us deserved.

My voice trembled, "Yes, Kimmie, everyone loves you. I love you very, very much. It's why we have to get you well; I just can't do anything without you."

Her head nodded up and down in agreement, "I know Mom; I'm your big helper, aren't I?"

"Dear God help us," I silently prayed while bending my head to kiss her forehead. I hoped to conceal from her eyes the heartbreak emanating from mine.

At exactly 10:30 a.m., nurses, pushing a stretcher, filled the room. Dan joined us, and we watched as they lifted Kimmie from the bed and onto the rolling, surgery gurney. The process involved difficult and time consuming procedures. The nurses were meticulously careful about not disturbing any of the tubes leading from her body.

Kim's terror-stricken eyes focused squarely upon us. She begged, "No more tests Mommy! No more, Daddy! Please! Please!"

The nurses allowed us to accompany Kim to the X-ray department. We walked beside her each step of the way. Dan somberly marched to Kim's left while gently stroking her arm. Holding her free hand, I walked on the right side of the gurney and softly reassured her as I squelched my own screams. "Kimmie, be brave, honey, just one more time. We need to find out what's making you sick. I love you baby."

The moment she saw the room with its huge machines; she began to cry in fear. The technicians in X-ray were well acquainted with our little girl by this time. Within seconds, one young man attempted to calm her by inquiring, "Kim, is your puppy's name Missy?"

She lay on the bed fighting back tears. "Huh ... huh, yes!"

A nurse asked, "Kim, who do you love?"

Through heart-rending sobs, Kimmie bravely recited her "Love Story."

"Uh-huh ... I love Mom ... huh-huh ... and I love Daddy ... uh- huh-huh ... and I love Dirkie ..."

Stop! Stop! Just let me take her home! Why can't I just swoop her up in my arms and carry her to safety?

I searched the cold, massive room. Threatening machines stood in all directions. Nothing in this room offered comfort. If I felt chills of fear, how frightening must it be for my Kimmie?

A nurse signaled it was time for us to leave. My heart sank; I drew in great breaths of air trying to steel myself before having to abandon my child one more time. I leaned over to give Kim a kiss and hug before gently stroking her hair and cheek. Dan's hand touched my shoulder. He silently urged me to let go by pressing his fingers into my flesh. When I reluctantly released my hold on Kim, Dan threw his arms about me for support when I began to sway at the screams.

"Mommy, don't leave me! Mommy, Daddy, don't leave me!"

Oh how those screams, those pleas for help, still ring in my ear!

Chapter 8 - Under His Sheltering Wings

Distraught over walking away from Kimmie, we stood in the hallway while I sobbed in Dan's arms.

"Babe, you've got to be strong. I don't want anything to happen to you or the baby today."

I wiped away my tears and gave my husband a crooked smile. "What do we do now?"

"Wait. It's all we *can* do. It'll be a long day." He took my hand, and we walked in silence toward the surgical waiting room to sit with our family and the many friends who had come to support us.

My parents and I elected to bring Dirk with us. Friends offered to care for him, but I couldn't entertain the thought of leaving him behind. His anxiety equaled ours, and I hoped his being in the company of his parents and both sets of grandparents would offer him a sense of security. As a result, the bevy of friends gathered around us took turns entertaining him with games, artwork, and trips to the coffee shop for treats.

For the first time since my arrival, Dan and I had time to talk. We found an isolated spot across the room where we could speak privately.

"Babe, Kimmie's never cried. I've never seen her shed one tear—until this morning when you walked into her room.

Somehow she's always managed to hold back the tears by telling everyone about our family and her puppy. Every nurse in ICU has heard Kim's "Love Story."

Dan clutched my hand, "I know you can't change anything, but just having you here makes everything seem better."

The lump in my throat momentarily prevented me from speaking. Kim's screams reverberated in the recesses of my mind. I choked back the threatening tears to reply. "It's better for me too. I'm devastated by the things I just witnessed and heard, but this is where I need to be. I saw Kimmie with my own eyes! I touched her, and held her hand. I thought I would lose my mind sitting at home having to depend on others to tell me about her."

Dan firmly squeezed my hand. "We have each other today."

My first glimpse of Kim sent a shiver of undulating fright down my spine. Her appearance portrayed in vivid detail the missing pieces of information withheld from me throughout the week. Dan's protective instincts sought to shield me, so he placed every minute detail of Kim's travail upon his own shoulders. Yet, my husband's face betrayed every reassurance he had offered. I sought words to comfort him.

"Honey, things are going to be okay. Don't ask me how I know this, but I am certain Kim will come through the tests and surgery today. I know everything will be all right."

Dan tightened his grip on my hand. "I hope so, but this week's been a nightmare. It's my first rodeo at waiting on tests, waiting on answers, and just plain waiting on who knows what! People come in and out of the room all day long. Not one of them ever has anything good to say. I don't think anybody knows sic 'em from sooey about what's wrong with her."

He stared into space momentarily before declaring, "It takes all I've got to stand still when the Doc comes in and talks about

Kimmie like she's a piece of meat laying on the table. If Dad hadn't been here, I don't know what I would have done. He kept repeating, 'Now, son, you need to stay calm.'"

Through gritted teeth, he whispered, "Even a blind hog finds an acorn once in a while, but I haven't found anything good in this!"

A great pause of silence followed. Dan had just broken his self-imposed protocol and lay bare the truth. Even now, I sensed he revealed the half, and not the whole, of the trauma he and Kimmie experienced.

Dear God, it's been worse than I have imagined!

I studied Dan's countenance. Gone was the carefree young man I met in college. In his place, sat a battle-weary veteran of a medical catastrophe supporting the full weight of our collapsed world on his shoulders. Words alluded me. I leaned forward and hugged the man whom I trusted with my life, and whispered, "I love you."

The day dripped endlessly by—one slow second at a time, but I could only keep repeating, "Everything will be all right."

For the first time in my life I understood the meaning of the words, "And the peace of God, which passeth all understanding, shall keep your hearts and minds through Christ Jesus" (Phil. 4:7 KJV).

I was at peace, completely calm with the knowledge Kim would survive the ordeal, but I had no basis of proof other than this fact: Jesus calmed my troubled heart and said to me, "It's all right."

Shortly after noon, Dan insisted, "Let's go to the cafeteria; you need to eat lunch."

My stomach balked at the thought of food, but I needed to keep my strength up for the baby's well-being. Just as we sat down at the table, Dan looked anxiously toward the entrance behind me, and jolted upright to his feet.

I swerved around in my chair. Dr. Carlton stood directly behind us with our pastor at his side. My heart pounded as the surgeon spoke with brevity and precision.

"I have found no evidence of a tumor. She is being prepared for surgery to implant the shunt. This could take several hours. I will inform you of the results as soon as the surgery is completed."

Before we could summon an acknowledgement, the doctor turned, and with great speed, exited the room.

Dan clutched me in a joyful hug. J.D., who had accompanied us, sat wiping tears while exclaiming, "That's wonderful! That's wonderful!"

Hour after hour laboriously crawled by while we alternately paced the halls and sat in the waiting room. Nurses and employees from every department in the hospital dropped by hourly to inquire about Kim. Their concern proved Kimmie had stolen the hearts of numerous people in a very short period of time. Each had heard about a little girl who told a beautiful "Love Story" to everyone she met.

The staff displayed concern for my health as well. Nurses who worked in the labor and delivery department dropped by to assure me they were prepared to act if I went into labor. Around three o'clock, the volunteer working in the waiting room scurried around until she found a small, unused lounge just steps away from the surgical ward. The room housed a large couch, along with several cushioned chairs.

"I want you to be comfortable," she insisted. "Now you have a place to lie down or put your feet up."

Dan, Dirk, Mother, and I, as well as a few friends were able to fit comfortably inside the room, and once again we settled in to await any news.

As each tiresome minute ticked by, I glanced at my watch. It's four-thirty—six long hours since the testing began! How much longer can this go on?

Hearing voices nearby, we bristled to attention. The doctor appeared in the doorway clad in green surgical clothes.

"She is fine," he immediately informed us.

We slumped into our chairs with relief washing over us.

"The shunt is working well and draining off the excess cerebral fluid. We haven't discovered the exact cause of her problem; I can only speculate it might be an unknown virus. If all goes well, your daughter should be home within two to three weeks, and then I will only need to see her periodically throughout the next year."

We stumbled to our feet while groping for words to properly thank him. Dan extended his hand toward the doctor, "Thank you! We, uh …"

"Thank you so much!" I added before the tears began to flow. Raw emotion made it impossible for either of us to speak.

Dr. Carlton nodded in apparent understanding, then abruptly exited the room. Dan and I held each other while we gave thanks to God, then hurriedly walked to the elevator. We couldn't wait to reach the Intensive Care Unit and our daughter.

Although her skin was pallid, and a white, gauze bandage covered her head, Kim looked exceptionally well. I whispered, "Kimmie, everything is okay. You'll feel better soon. Daddy and Mommy are here sweetie. We love you."

She struggled to open her eyes, but the effects of the

anesthetic overpowered her. We were content to know she was alive and on her way to a full recovery.

I stood beside Kim caressing her hand, when from the corner of my eye, I spotted a brown, paper bag taped to the end of her bed. Curious, I walked toward the bag and read the words, "HAIR, DO NOT DESTROY." The words soared toward me like arrows aimed directly at my heart. I assumed her head would be shaved for the surgery, but the reality of it never fully penetrated my thoughts. Too many other fears dominated my thinking.

How could I ever possibly explain this to Kim? I thought of those wispy bangs and the soft swirl of blond curls gently tapering to her shoulders. Tears welled. I remembered the day her bangs were first trimmed. She looked in the mirror, smiled infectiously, and proudly announced, "Now I have bangs just like you Mom."

I envisioned her stepping out of the bathtub, putting on a nightgown, brushing her hair, and then running into the living room to find Dan. I saw the image of Kim giving her father a quick hug before twirling around in a circle in front of him. "Daddy, aren't I pretty?" she asked.

Just before Christmas, our little tomboy, who endearingly followed in the steps of her big brother, suddenly blossomed into a frilly little girl. Each day she carefully brushed her hair while looking in the mirror, then twirled toward me. "Mom, can I please have some of your lipstick and powder?"

When Dirk sought quiet time playing with his trucks, Kim disappeared for extended periods of time to rummage through my closet. With her feet clad in a pair of my best heels, she clomped-clomped her way into the living room wearing one of my dresses. The long skirt puddled on the floor and trailed behind her, while strands of pearls encircled her neck. Lipstick and perfume completed every ensemble.

I shuddered at the prospect of Kim being forced to wait endless months until her hair grew long enough to brush again. It's strange how the mind will find such a small and insignificant problem to dwell upon when the most important thing of all is life. I chided myself. Kim is alive; she will be home again in a few weeks! Yet, to my dismay, I cried for her lost hair.

The ICU staff allowed us to stay with her for more than an hour before the nurse on duty informed us, "Your visitation time has exceeded the limit, and I must ask you to leave."

She reminded Dan, "Kim needs her rest, and her mother needs to follow the same advice."

I didn't want to leave; I didn't feel tired at all. I just wanted to be with Kim when she woke up. But the nurse would not budge in spite of my protests, and we grudgingly left to rejoin the family.

While visiting with my parents, Dan made plans to ride home with us. "The nurses aren't going to let me stay with Kim tonight. This might be my only chance to go home for more clothes and to get my truck. My folks can't stay past Sunday, so I need to have my own vehicle. I can get things rounded up tonight and be back here before visiting hours begin in the morning."

Before leaving, we drew upon God's strength to say goodbye to Kim. When Dan and I saw her for the second time, she rested quietly in a deep sleep. We were relieved to see her sleeping so peacefully after watching her suffer over the past week, and so I felt somewhat better about having to leave. Now my main focus must be to give birth to a healthy baby and get back to Kim as quickly as possible.

At exactly 8:00 p.m., a voice announced over the intercom, "Visitation time is now over. Please exit the patient rooms."

We reluctantly kissed our sweet child farewell while a nurse stood in the doorway waiting to usher us out.

I stopped midway down the hall, and turned back toward the ICU. "Dan, I can't do this. I can't leave Kimmie all by herself! There's a couch in the lounge. I can lie down there, but I have to stay here!"

"Babe, I've tried that. In about fifteen minutes, these doors will be locked. They won't let anyone stay up here at night."

"Then I'll sit outside the door. I can't leave my baby!"

"Listen; that nun, who's a nurse, is tough as nails. If she had a broom, she'd either ride it, or take one swipe with it and knock us out of here. She doesn't put up with any sass. I fought her the first night, and lost when she threatened to get security.

"Hon, I know you don't want to leave. I don't want to either. My gut churns every night about this time, but you're not gonna be able to stay. On top of that, you've got to take care of yourself. Dr. Park wants you back home tonight. At least I can make sure you get home safe."

Tears streamed down my cheeks as I stared at the door. Why can't anything ever be easy?

"Come on Babe. We need to leave before that nurse finds her broom."

Our final task involved finding proper words to thank Dan's parents. Mary lovingly cared for Kim throughout the week, and comforted her in my place. J.D. served as a bedrock of support for his son. I couldn't find the words to express how much I loved them for what they had done. "Mary, thank you so much for—

"Now, you know we wouldn't have had it any other way,"

Mary interrupted. "We love Kimmie. We wanted to be here with her!"

Mary and J.D. planned to spend the night in another's son's home just ten minutes from the hospital. If any emergency occurred during the night, they would be close by. Our plans were settled, and the time for our departure arrived.

Panic assailed me. I quickly excused myself and darted to the nearest restroom. While panting, I silently screeched, "O God! O God! I can't leave my baby! I can't abandon her again! Lord, help me! Watch over her dear Jesus!"

His peace descended upon me as a soft whisper in the night, and I calmly exited the room and rejoined my family.

My heart broke at the thought of Kim being left all alone in the ICU without anyone she loved beside her, but I could not change the rules. I could only depend upon God's love to keep her through the dark hours before dawn.

After saying our goodbyes, traveling home, and gathering up Dan's supplies, it was almost one o'clock in the morning before we exhaustedly slumped into bed. Sleep alluded me. My mind raced through the day's events. I replayed and treasured each of Kim's sweet words. She just had to be okay; after all, hadn't God promised me everything would be all right?

CHAPTER 9 - WAVES OF FEAR AND FRIENDS OF PRAYER

I rose long before the sun appeared in the east. Dan needed clothes laundered, and I needed something to keep me busy. As things turned out, he didn't have time to wait for his shirts to dry. Shortly before six in the morning, the phone rang. I hurried to answer it, and screeched, "Hello!"

"This is Dr. Carlton. May I speak with Mr. Grissom?

I covered the phone with my hand, "Dan! Hurry! It's the doctor!"

Swallowing the growing lump in my throat, I breathlessly panted a trembling response into the receiver, "This is Mrs. Grissom speaking."

Dan lunged toward the extension, and we each gaped in horror while simultaneously hearing the doctor's report.

"Mrs. Grissom, Kim's intracranial pressure is greater than before; the shunt is not working."

Those were the last words I heard. Dan completed the conversation with the doctor while I stood shrieking, "No! No! No!"

Mother ran from the kitchen, and walked me to the bedroom. I screamed for what seemed like an eternity, "Please God; please don't let Kim suffer any more! Oh, dear God, I can't take it!"

But heartaches don't disappear simply because we are too afraid to face them. I survived everything thrown my way in the early morning hours … not because of my great inner strength … but because of God's strength working through me. Swiftly, his love wiped away the tears and gave my soul calm assurance with the words, "Everything's all right."

By the time I was calm enough to speak, Dan stood beside me ready to leave. Dr. Carlton warned, "The shunt must be removed and relocated. We'll prep her for surgery. You need to get here as soon as possible to sign the surgical release forms."

Dan immediately gathered his clothes, stuffed his wallet into his back pocket, and grabbed his keys. Before bolting out the door, he pulled me into his arms for a quick embrace … and once again I was left behind. I allowed myself to become too upset for anyone to think of letting me make the trip; and just as in the preceding days, I could do nothing other than pray and wait for news.

I stood watch at the door until his truck disappeared from sight, then took one last gulp of air to brace myself against unwanted tears. I ducked my head, and turned around hoping to avoid any conversation with my parents, and gazed straight into the eyes of my son.

The flurry of activity surrounding Dan's sudden departure both awakened and alarmed Dirk. I saw the terror etched upon his face; yet he stood at attention like the good little soldier he had become, and quietly waited for me.

Dear God, what can I tell him? I didn't attempt to offer hollow words or empty reassurances. He was much too perceptive for half-truths. Instead, I simply gathered him into my arms and held him tightly.

"Mom, do I have to go to school today? I don't want to go. I want to stay here with you!"

I looked into his questioning eyes and knew regardless of what others advised, school would not be a distraction for Dirk. If my heart was shattered, his must be splintered and bleeding. He could no more go to class and forget about the things happening miles away than I could stay in this house and pretend all was well. I said a quick prayer of thanksgiving for Mrs. Richards, the school principle, who had been so kind when I spoke with her. "Don't worry about anything," she assured. "Dirk is a smart little boy. He can easily catch up on anything he misses."

I gathered him into my arms and answered, "No, honey. You can stay here with me. We need each other today."

Just before Dad left to follow Dan to the hospital, he inquired, "Can I do anything for you baby?"

Dad had worked hard all of his life, and for most of those years, he suffered with chronic heart problems. His once dark hair now held streaks of grey, but this decorated veteran of the Second World War remained a giant in my eyes.

Looking up, I touched his work-roughened hand and asked, "Would you call one of the deacons and request prayers from the church members?"

He softly squeezed my shoulder in response before leaving to make the call.

The news spread rapidly, and church friends streamed into my parents' home to offer assistance and comforting words. The phone rang constantly. Hoping for a report on Kim, I answered each call on the first ring, but I heard nothing from Dan. Instead, we received call upon call from people throughout the community pledging prayers for our family.

Coincidently, on this particular day, the women of our church were having an all-day mission study. Every half-hour, one of the women stepped out of the study area to check for any news about Kim. One participant confided, "We tried to study the book, but the Lord kept pulling our minds from the book and toward Kim. We alternately prayed and studied from early morning to late afternoon."

I find it impossible to express how much we needed those prayers. It's one thing to pray alone, and quite another to have others praying with you. The prayers of these wonderful ladies sustained us. Without their support, we would have broken under the strain.

I can only guess at the amount of mental anguish Dan endured throughout the day. He awoke to the news of Kim's need for immediate surgery. While he hurriedly dressed and threw his things in a bag, I sat on the bed sobbing uncontrollably. Afterward, I felt such shame because I couldn't hold back the tears for his sake. When he needed me the most, I broke into tiny pieces before his eyes. Where was my faith when I really needed it?

Dan virtually raced against time. He sped over the curving roads to the hospital, and rushed into Kimmie's room only to find her in successive seizures.

My husband avoided hospitals like the plague. He hated both the significance and the confinement of hospitals. The past week had been literal torment for him while he stayed beside Kim in my absence. He could not bear to watch her suffer with a headache. Now he sat helplessly watching our daughter writhe and jerk uncontrollably with convulsions.

Dr. Carlton stated, "With this type of episode, the patient is never aware of the event."

Nevertheless, watching her must have been sheer agony. Mary later told me, "At one point, Dan was afraid of not only losing Kim, but you and the baby as well. In his darkest moments, he despairingly repeated, 'Mom, I don't know what I will do if I lose all three of them!'"

I did this to Dan. Because of my lack of faith, I gave him cause to worry about my life, and the life of our unborn child, as well as Kim's. Yet, I give praise unto the Lord. God is sufficient to meet all our needs. He provided us with strength and benevolently brought each of us through the turbulent morning and the second surgery.

Six hours later, Dan called. "Everything is fine. Kim's in recovery and doing well. I should be able to see her in a few minutes."

I hung up the phone, thanked God for his mercy, then stepped outside for some fresh air. Two ladies from our church were playing catch with Dirk in the front yard. I briefly averted my eyes. He should be racing and playing with Kim, but the days when my children laughed and played together had come to a screeching halt. Oh Lord, why has everything been smashed to smithereens?

I blinked back the threatening tears, and silently mouthed "Thank you" to the women who were running after the ball Dirk had thrown near the curb. Because of our children's special bond, Dirk's anxiety was building. He missed Kim terribly. In a matter of days, our reserved "little man" had evolved into a fidgety, hyperactive child.

When he entered kindergarten, Kim was crushed because she couldn't go to school with her big brother. From morning until midafternoon of each school day, she constantly inquired, "Is it time to go get Dirk?"

Although Dirk's voice was becoming lost in the maze of confusion surrounding us, I saw a similar plea in his troubled eyes: *"When is Kim coming home?"* But Jesus saw his need and sent beautiful women of God to give him special attention.

Just before nightfall, Dad returned from the hospital. I met him at the door to quiz him for information, but I received the answer I would repeatedly hear over the following days, "She is restless."

I never knew exactly what Dan and other family members were describing with the word, *"restless."* I assumed they chose this word explicitly to avoid causing me further alarm by describing Kim's constant struggle with pain.

At ten o'clock, I crawled into bed. I lay looking up at the ceiling—tired, tense, and anxious. We could no longer circumvent the great possibility of brain damage. The human brain can withstand only so much pressure, and certainly the seizures had not been to Kim's advantage.

New worries and fears began to surface, but I needed to put each of these thoughts aside so I could rest. I knew this was the appointed night for our baby to enter the world. Without any obvious signs of beginning labor; I simply felt the Holy Spirit giving me an advanced warning. The matter was settled in my heart.

CHAPTER 10 - GOD'S BLESSING AMID HEARTACHE

SATURDAY, FEBRUARY 23

At five o'clock in the morning, I woke Mother, and asked her to drive me to the hospital. I tearfully kissed my son and left him in Dad's care. This didn't resemble my plan for the birth of our third child. I lay alone in the delivery room with only brief visits from the nurses to interrupt the silence. Dan wasn't beside me to hold my hand or pace nervously back and forth across the room. Only my Savior stood at my side to keep vigil with me.

The labor went comparatively easy. Dr. Paul arrived to examine me and then announced, "The baby is in the breech position, so it's going to be a long labor. I'm going to get a cup of coffee, and I'll see you a little later."

Fear stabbed at my heart. The baby is in the breech position! I've never heard of anyone having a breech birth without surgery!

I didn't have long to ponder these thoughts. Without warning, an intense pain shuddered through my body. Dr. Paul never had time to drink his cup of coffee. A nurse placed a mask upon my face and told me to take a deep breath. I knew nothing else until shortly after eight o'clock in the morning. By

God's grace, the baby was delivered without surgery. When I awoke, the doctor announced, "It's a girl."

A girl? My head began to whirl. The two church ladies had me convinced this baby was a little boy. The three of us must have forgotten to consult God.

Before I could take it all in, the nurse placed the baby in my arms. My heart swelled with love when I saw her for the first time. She looked exactly like Kim and Dirk had as newborns. She owned the same Cupid's bow mouth, snubbed nose, and blue eyes of her older siblings at birth. Our three children differed only in the color of their hair. The baby's hair resembled the color of golden wheat, while Kim and Dirk had blond, bordering on white hair, at birth. As I snuggled the blanket securely around the baby, her tiny hand gripped my little finger, and I knew for certain this was the child God meant us to have.

Exhaustion crept over me. I drifted in and out of sleep throughout most of the day. Dan startled me awake when he came for a brief visit midafternoon. He traveled the ninety-minute distance just to see and hold his newborn daughter.

"I think she's a keeper," he said with a twinkle in his eye.

As we spoke with one another, I realized his thoughts were the same as mine. The nurses brought the baby to me for feedings throughout the day. Savoring the sweetness of God's beautiful gift, I held this precious child in my arms. She was perfect in every way, but somehow it all seemed surreal.

Dan expressed my feelings so well. "Honey, the baby is a beautiful little doll; she's what we've been waiting for. I love her, but our other baby is seventy-five miles away in another hospital. I want all three of our kids here—at home with us!"

Tears fell when I shamefully admitted feeling the same way. This was supposed to be a day filled with happiness. The baby lying in the nursery was a sweet blessing, but my heart was torn between Kim and the new life we were given. I searched my husband's countenance; his haggard appearance revealed an inner turmoil.

"Dan, I need to know about Kim."

Disinclined to give me any news, he shook his head.

"Please! You have to tell me the truth."

He chewed on his lower lip before answering. "Kim's still restless; she can't sleep, and she jerks and thrashes around on the bed. The doctor's afraid to give her anything to calm her down, so we just have to wait."

"Wait for what?"

He paused while groping for the right words, then with a barely audible voice answered. "Now, don't get upset, but Dr. Carlton thinks Kim might have a rare disease in which the gray and the white matter of the brain are allergic to one another."

"What? How can parts of the brain be allergic to each other?"

Shaking his head in disbelief, Dan slowly mumbled, "I don't know Babe. But ... if she has this disease, then one part of the brain will destroy the other."

My head dropped in sheer horror at this monstrous possibility. I couldn't comprehend anything so horrifying. My mind resisted the very idea of this happening to our daughter.

"No! It can't be true! She's gone through a tremendous ordeal. Maybe she only needs time to heal. If I could just be with her—"

"We don't know she *has* the disease; they don't have a way to detect it yet. There are too many other things to rule out first. Dr. Carlton's giving her medicine to reduce the swelling in her brain, and we're hoping it will help."

Hoping? Instinctively, I knew he was holding something

back. "Dan, I need to know the truth about Kim; it can't be any worse than lying here imagining all sorts of things."

He grasped my hand. His thumb rubbed back and forth across my knuckles while he searched for his next words. "The tests show Kim has brain damage."

Looking away, I fluttered my lashes to prevent any tears. My mind flashed back to Dirk's first day of kindergarten. While I helped him locate his assigned desk and hurriedly placed his supplies in the proper bins, I suddenly missed Kim. I looked around the room, and found her sitting in the midst of other children happily putting together puzzles designed for much older children.

Kim, months away from her third birthday, correctly placed the puzzle pieces together without the slightest bit of trouble. She beamed with delight, and I regretted having to pull her away from the table when the time came for us to leave. Each morning after this experience she begged, "Mom, I want to go to school with Dirk so I can play with the puzzles."

From an early age, Kim displayed advanced skills. She spoke in complete sentences at the age of fifteen months, and her determination at such an early age shocked us. She worked diligently at every task until she had it mastered, and rarely asked for help with anything. If anyone gave unsolicited assistance, she complained, "I can do it myself."

Now, the future looked uncertain. I cried, not for myself, but for Kim. How could life be so cruel as to take such a bright child and leave her either physically or mentally disabled? What kind of life would Kim have if she could no longer play and run with Dirk? How would she be affected if others must assist her with the things she loved doing for herself? I didn't want this life for my daughter, and my heart broke at the thought of it.

Dan reminded me of what was truly important. "Babe, it

doesn't make any difference. She's still our sweet little Kimmie, and we will love her and take care of her for the rest of our lives."

He looked toward me, waiting for confirmation I had heard and agreed with what he said. Shamed by my thoughts, I choked out the words, "Yes, of course we will love her and take care of her, no matter what!"

It no longer mattered whether she would be the same as before. Kim was alive! Our love for her was unchanging. We would willingly take care of her, and protect her from the world.

I meant each of those words, but my heart rejected the prospect of any permanent damage. I held onto the one thin line of hope available to me. Kim's young age was an advantage. Any damaged tissue could be healed with time and therapy.

"Honey," I insisted. "I know Kim will be all right. God has comforted me too many times with those words. They must be true. Everything she's endured must be for some purpose. Perhaps it's so people can witness a miracle of God, but she will be okay."

Tears welled in his eyes as Dan struck the final blow. "The doctor says Kim has a fifty-fifty chance."

CHAPTER 11 - PASSIONATE PLEAS

After saying goodbye to my weary and heartsick husband, Dan's last words hammered at me. His visit lasted mere moments; he feared being away from Kim for any great length of time. He came only to see the baby whose birth he had missed.

I attempted to pray, but the words stuck in my throat. I cupped my hands over my face to shut out the world while silently petitioning the Lord. "Please God, hold Kim in your arms and comfort her in my place. Let her know how much I love her."

"What's wrong?"

Startled, I looked upward. My mother stood at the entrance to the room with one hand pushing against the door.

"Dan was just here. Kim's reports aren't good." Ending with Kim's chances of survival, I repeated the information he gave me.

Mother sat in the chair beside my bed absorbing each bitter detail. I noted the sadness in her eyes, but her words belied any grief. "It won't do Kim any good for you to get so upset. You need to stay calm and get well so you can go take care of her."

"I know; I wish I could stop worrying, but it's all I can think about! Mother, I need to pray, but I don't think I can get the words out. Would you please call one of the deacons and ask for prayer?"

"I think there's a phone in the lobby I can use. I'll call Cliff and Leon."

My thoughts weighed heavy upon my soul, but my faith lay in the promise Jesus gave long ago: "Again I say unto you, that if two of you shall agree on earth as touching anything that they shall ask, it shall be done for them of my Father which is in heaven. For where two or three are gathered together in my name, there am I in the midst of them" (Matt.18:19–20 KJV).

Surely greater power was available when more than one entered into prayer with God. Within minutes, Brother Cliff, and my mother, along with Brother Leon and his wife, Ruby, entered the room and knelt around my hospital bed to intercede on Kim's behalf. We asked God to grant her the rest she needed, and to give her writhing body peace. When the prayer ended, a calm assurance of God's presence surrounded us. Dan later informed me Kim fell asleep within a few hours following our prayer and slept peacefully throughout the night. Praise God!

SUNDAY, FEBRUARY 24

I held my sweet one-day-old infant. She was the epitome of God's beautiful handiwork. How was it possible to be blessed with such a precious baby on the eighth day of our nightmare? How could I ever forage the strength to leave her?

"How are you two doing?" Dad inquired from the doorway.

I looked up in surprise. "We're both doing well. Why are you here so early? You should be on your way to church."

"Well, your mama and I are driving up to see Kim today. We're taking Dirk with us. They're outside, waiting for me in the car. I just wanted to tell you where we will be so you won't worry."

Dad's brief visit revived my spirits. I hoped Kim might

respond more readily to my mother's presence. "Please dear God, give Mother the ability to comfort Kim."

I waited impatiently for my parents' return and news of Kim. Mother's longtime friend, Ruby, sat with me throughout the entire afternoon. Determined to keep my mind occupied, she talked nonstop for hours, but her valiant efforts failed to divert my thoughts.

"Oh Lord Jesus, please take care of Kim," I silently repeated throughout the day.

Shortly after five o'clock, Mother timidly entered my room. "I couldn't do much for Kim. I'm not certain she recognized me or your daddy."

Mustering the strength to extinguish the last of my hopes, Mother absently smoothed the blanket on the bed, and tucked it around me. "I don't think Kim is really aware of anything."

I stuffed the report further inside my heart to pull out and think about later. I needed to get out of bed and walk to the lobby. Dirk stood at the nursery window peering at our family's newest member. I gathered him into my arms for a hug. "What do you think about your new little sister?"

"She's little," he answered.

"Yes, babies are little at first, but they grow really fast. She reminds me of how both you and Kim looked when you were tiny babies."

"What's her name?"

"Daddy and I decided to name her Kristi."

"Does she have blue eyes like Kim?"

"She does right now; we'll have to wait and see whether they change to brown later as yours did. Kim's eyes never changed color; they just became a more sparkly blue."

"Kim's eyes make you look at her," he replied.

"God designs each of us in a different way. That's what makes you so special."

We sat down on a bench in the hallway. Dirk snuggled beside me. His haunting eyes seared mine. "Mom, they didn't let me see Kim today."

I gently squeezed his hand. "I know honey. I'm sorry. Hospitals have rules about children visiting sick people."

"But, I'm bigger than Kim."

"The rules say you must be twelve years old before you can go into the halls of the hospital. They don't want you to get sick too."

"I don't like their rules!"

"Neither do I. We both miss Kim. I want to see her too."

"Mom, do you remember the night we played 'Bronco Busting' with Dad before Kim got sick?"

"Yes honey; I do. I've never laughed so much in my life. Dad got down on his hands and knees, and the two of you jumped on his back. Kim sat in front holding on to Dad's shirt collar while you grabbed his belt. He bucked and bucked, and you two almost fell off, but you both kept holding on even though you were riding sideways.

"I will never forget Dad's high-pitched squeal, just before he collapsed on the floor. 'You're choking me!'"

"That was fun, Mom."

Dirk paused before posing his second question. "When Kim gets well, do you think we can have a picnic in the back yard?"

"You mean like we did last summer?"

"Yes."

"Hmm," I reminisced. "Nothing better than eating hot dogs and cookies on a blanket under the old elm tree."

"And then we raced!"

"Oh, yes! Anytime you and Kim are outside for any length of time, you race."

"Do you think we can go on walks too?"

His soulful eyes reflected a great yearning. He wanted our lives to be as they were before our world crashed. "Well, it's getting warmer every day honey. I think it would be a great idea. We had lots of fun just talking, laughing, and spending time together."

"Yeah, Kim always grabbed your hand when we crossed the street and said, 'Mom, you better hold my hand so I won't get run over.'"

"Yes, and she always wanted you to walk close beside her as well"

"Sometimes we even walked all the way to Gran and Bob's store." Dirk averted his eyes. "Now I go there every day."

I pushed back the lump in my throat. *Don't let him see your fear.* "Honey, I know things are so different for you right now. Dad and I are going to do everything we can to get Kim well and bring her home so we can all be together again."

The floor nurse appeared in the hall. "Visitation hour is over. It's feeding time for the babies."

I peered into Dirk's sad eyes. "I'm sorry we didn't get to see each other very long today. Dad and I love you very much. Kim loves you too. Hopefully, she will be much better soon, and you can visit her."

I bestowed one last hug upon my son before he and my parents left the hospital. "I'll see you again tomorrow. I love you!"

Alone in my room after feeding Kristi, I silently thanked God for his mercy and asked for forgiveness. A voice inside my head frequently blamed God for allowing these events to take place at a time when I physically could not travel to be with

Kim. In the moonlit stillness, the Holy Spirit revealed to me God's greater love which goes beyond our immediate needs.

My circumstances had nothing to do with my physical limitations. I lacked the ability to keep my emotions in check while watching Kim suffer through such pain, endure all the frightening tests, and writhe with endless seizures. Unable in my weakness to support or comfort her, I would have crumbled under the pressure, and added to her anxieties.

God knows us better than we know ourselves. Although at times I still feel cheated because I could not be with her throughout the week of her surgery, I am grateful Dan and his parents were there to comfort Kimmie. Mary possesses the unique ability to separate herself from highly charged emotions and perform the necessary, giving empathy when needed and remaining stalwart in the face of difficulties. Kim needed her grandmother during the dark moments.

MONDAY, FEBRUARY 25

I anxiously awaited my dismissal from the hospital, but Dr. Paul insisted I remain in the hospital one more day. "Your blood pressure is too low. We need to take care of that before I dismiss you. And … you didn't exactly have a routine delivery."

"But, Dr. Paul, I—"

"I know what you're planning to do. As soon as you're dismissed, you'll go straight to the hospital to stay with Kim. I'm going to make sure you are well enough to stand up to the task before I sign your release. Nurses have noted the times when you've been too weak to hold your baby. You're in this for the long haul. You don't want to end up back here in this bed—too sick to take care of yourself or Kim!"

No amount of protesting on my part changed his decision.

Obviously, the nurses saw through my efforts to hide my lingering fatigue. I tried to rest, but my mind never ceased its worry. Instead, I spent the day praying for Kim.

Within minutes following the baby's two o'clock feeding, Dan appeared in the doorway and strode across the room. He hastily bent down to gather me into his arms before quickly bestowing a kiss. His haunting eyes were conspicuous with anguish. He no longer possessed his former bold and confident demeanor.

"I think Kim's doing a little better," he said. "She's more alert. I promised her I would find out when you were coming to stay with her."

"Honey, I'm leaving this hospital tomorrow whether Dr. Paul releases me or not!"

"I want you and the baby to be okay before you're dismissed, but—"

Dan's lips blew out a shuddering breath. "Kimmie needs you! She never stops asking about you. It's killing me because I can't give her what she wants!"

Rivulets of tears fell from my eyes. Why, oh why am I stuck in this hospital bed?

Had it been possible, my heart would have broken into a thousand pieces when he implored, "Babe, all Kimmie ever talks about is seeing you. If you could just get there … if you could just be with her … I know she would be all right!"

He confirmed my deepest thoughts: If I could just get there, Kim would be fine! "Dan, I promise I will be there tomorrow as quickly as things can be arranged!"

He left within fifteen minutes of his arrival. Patient phones were not available at that time, so he drove each of those long miles just to keep his promise to Kim. A father's love has no boundaries.

From the moment Dan exited the room, my lips spoke one constant prayer throughout the night and into the new dawn. "Lord, just hold onto Kim. Please God, if you will just take care of her until I can get there, I know I can pull her out of this. Oh Lord, just please give me time to get to the hospital. She needs me so much Lord; please keep her safe!"

I used the two most frightening words in a Christian's vocabulary in my prayer, *I* and *me*. We often forget just how small and powerless we are. In my arrogance, I neatly planned out the solution to our problem. Upon my arrival at the hospital, I intended to take Kim into my arms, and just as though she had a skinned knee, I would kiss her and make her well. A mother's love can do many things, but it cannot heal. Restoring the body is a province left only to God. My realization of this fact came all too quickly.

Chapter 12 - God's Strength, My Weakness

Tuesday's dawning crept in, and the baby and I were dismissed from the hospital. I sat alone when I signed the birth certificate form and wrote the name, Kristi Lynne, in the space provided. Memories of the births of our other two children filtered through my brain, and tears fell on the paper. This precious child deserved the same devoted attention from both of her parents, but I was alone during labor and delivery, and I sat alone completing the final details. I shook my head. It served no purpose to dwell on things I could not change. Both Dan and I were doing the things required to take care of our family.

In a few hours, Dad planned to drive me to the hospital, but a myriad of tasks must be accomplished in the meantime. Mother drove me to our home so we could gather all of the baby's things. We boxed bottles, formula, diapers, blankets, and clothes; the list seemed endless, but Mother needed each of these items to care for an infant. I rifled through drawers and closets, packing a bag for myself before we took pictures of our newborn.

God blessed our lives with wonderful parents. I didn't need to ask whether Mother was willing to care for Dirk and three-day-old Kristi. We had an unspoken understanding. Both she and Dad opened up their home to our children for however long Kim's hospitalization lasted.

My heart splintered at the thought of leaving them. I never doubted the baby would be well loved and cared for, but we needed this time to bond, and Dirk now lived in a confused and heartsick world. In one short day, all of the attention abruptly diverted to Kim. Although he understood the circumstances, he was frightened for his sister's life. My leaving heightened his sense of abandonment.

I drew him closer to me while we sat together on Mother's couch. Dirk's smile could light up the state of Texas, but sadness extinguished the twinkling light from his eyes, and his lips no longer parted with a smile.

"Honey, I love you so much, and I am very proud of you for being such a big boy while Kim has been in the hospital. I don't want to leave you and your new little sister, but I need to go to the hospital and stay with Kim. She is sick, and she needs me to take care of her."

Furiously defying any pent up tears to flow, he rubbed his eyes while nodding his head in agreement. My hand gently brushed away the soft blond hair from his eyes before I kissed his forehead. I loved my brave and stalwart son more than I thought possible.

"I need you to be really good for Gran and Bob while I'm gone, and please help them take care of the baby. Kim misses you and wants to be here with you, so I'm going to do everything I can to help her get well.

"Dirk, do you remember when you taught Kim how to ride her tricycle, and the proper way to hold Missy? You also taught her the best places to hide too, and when Santa gave you a swing set, you followed Kim up the steps of the slide so she wouldn't fall. You're a wonderful big brother, and she loves you very much."

"Yeah, and Kim thinks she needs to take care of me too. She always tries to put a blanket on me when I lay on the floor to watch TV."

Smiling through tears, I agreed. "Yes, she tugs and pulls Grandma's afghan from the couch and says, 'Here Dirkie, you better let me cover you up so you won't get cold.' Kim's the little mother hen of the family, and you are our very brave little man. Always remember I love you with all my heart. You will be in my prayers every night."

While I held Dirk securely in my arms, his chest shuddered. He choked back any threatening sobs before answering, "Take care of Kim, Mom."

I clutched him to my heart while answering his plea, "I promise to take very good care of her. I'm taking pictures of you and the baby with me. I know she will love being able to see your smile every day."

Shaking with anxiety, I rose from the couch, walked over to the yellow-laced bassinet, and looked upon our sleeping newborn. How could I leave her? Kristi was our family's much anticipated gift from God. Kim loved this baby long before her birth. She anxiously awaited the baby's arrival, thanking God each night for "our baby."

Now the infant God sent us lay swaddled in a lace-ruffled cradle, but Kim was miles away from home fighting for her own life. I wanted to scream at the injustice, but instead, the Holy Spirit reminded me of a better way to honor my children.

Kimmie couldn't be here to bow her head and press her tiny hands together to form a steeple, so instead, I placed my hand on Kristi's forehead and silently repeated Kim's sweet daily prayer.

"Thank you God, for our food. And thank you for Mommy and Daddy, and for Dirkie, and for Granny and Pawpaw, and for Grandma and Grandpa, and for Missy. And thank you for our baby."

Cherishing the moment, I held Kristi's tiny hand in mine. Mother quietly slipped beside me. Groping for words to convey my gratitude, I looked toward her and stammered, "Mother, I ... uh ... thank you—"

Before I could say another word, she stiffened her spine as if for battle and replied, "You go on; your Daddy's waiting. We'll be okay."

These no-nonsense words from the most courageous woman I have ever known, gave me the strength to turn from my sleeping infant, give Dirk one last, long hug, and rush out the door.

I waited impatiently for the car to travel each long mile. It seemed as though the road, and the recently lowered speed limit from seventy to fifty-five miles per hour, were deliberately keeping me from getting to Kim. I sat clenching my hands into fists while silently thinking if Dad would just let me get out of the car, I could run to the hospital faster than this vehicle was traveling! Just before one o'clock, I saw the outline of the hospital in the distance; my heart trembled in anticipation.

Dan must have been on the fourth floor pacing outside of ICU, and watching from the windows, because he arrived downstairs just as Dad and I entered the hospital. Despair plastered his face. He greeted me with an impassioned plea of regret.

"I wish you could have gotten here a few hours earlier. Kim was much better this morning. I took her for a walk around the room. She was pretty unsteady on her feet. I held on to both of her hands, and helped her like we did when she was first learning to walk, but she managed about fifteen steps.

"Each time Kim took a step, she looked up at me and asked, 'Daddy, when is Mom coming?' I promised her you'd be coming soon, but now, I just don't know..."

Shaking his head in distress, he lamented, "Something has happened to her. Our baby's gone again."

My heart stopped. No! No! No! Once more, I had lost precious moments I could never reclaim. Lord, why couldn't I get here yesterday?

The three of us sprinted to the elevator, and counted each second until we reached the fourth floor, then charged down the long corridor to her room. With each step, I silently asked God to give me courage. The door swung open, and there lay my child with a nurse standing watch on each side of her bed.

Desperately needing to feel those tiny fingers clasped around my neck and to hear the words, "Mom, I love you," I ran toward Kim. To my horror, she never turned her head in my direction. The sound of my voice could not summon even the slightest hint of recognition on her face.

What had happened? Only a few hours earlier, Kim walked and talked with her daddy. Now she lay on the bed with her head jerking back and forth while she uttered the same, "Uh-uh, Uh-uh," over and over. Her legs and arms thrashed wildly about on the bed while hitting the steel guard rails. Was this the *restless* everyone reported to me?

I leaned over the bed and attempted to put my arms around Kim to offer comfort, but her head jerked away and her eyes stared in the opposite direction. Arms and legs flailed against me. Like a marionette, Kim's limbs were being maneuvered by an outside force compelling her body to move in opposition to her will. My child existed somewhere in this maze, and I had to reach her!

I tried everything. I sang to her; I spoke softly to her. In desperation, I showed her pictures of Dirk and the baby. Surely the sight of these two could reach Kimmie, but sadly, nothing worked.

In mere moments I learned a bitter lesson. I had prayed for days. Each time I asked God to take care of Kim until I could be with her. I was conceited enough to believe I could work a miracle. How terribly wrong I had been! With abrupt clarity, I realized I could do nothing. I stood absolutely powerless to offer my child anything. My love could not bring about a miraculous healing.

Saddened and grieved over the turn of events, Dad left shortly after our arrival. Dan and I stood vigil beside Kim for hours in defiance of the rules—afraid to leave for even one second. Our minds scanned a full gamut of reasons for her distress, from the probability of jealousy over the baby, to the possibility of a reaction to the medication.

The doctor appeared on his evening rounds. He addressed me first. "How did Kim react to your arrival?"

I attempted to rid the hurt from my voice before answering, "She didn't acknowledge me."

I didn't want anyone to know how totally lost I felt. After my abrupt abandonment of Kim, she just might not *want* to acknowledge my presence. I knew nothing about the medical aspect of the brain, and no one could explain her actions. I only knew two things for certain: My child would not look at me, and she could not speak.

"I'm going to order a new medication," the doctor stated. "We'll see if it brings about a change before morning."

As the night approached, we were forced to leave Kim in

the care of the nurses. I wanted so desperately to stay. I never wanted to leave her again, but the rules for Intensive Care were rigid, and Dan insisted I needed rest to face the next day.

As we exited the room, I prayed, "Lord, please keep Kim through the night; hold her safe in your arms."

Dan's brother invited us to stay in his home while Kim was hospitalized, and since Gary and his wife lived only minutes from the hospital, we went there for the night. Sleep refused to descend upon either of us. Dan worried about the hospital and doctor bills, his closed business, and most importantly, Kim. I don't know whether my fear for her life, or my own self-pity, cost me the most sleep. My thoughts and emotions twisted in my mind until I could not separate the two.

I simply could not imagine life without Kim, so I rejected the very idea of losing her. My mind skipped back and forth over these thoughts, but it invariably came back to dwell upon one fact: I was virtually incapable of doing one thing to help my child. My pride declared she needed nothing other than me, but this situation unequivocally proved me wrong. She did not need me, and in fact, she might not even know me.

CHAPTER 13 - MOMMY'S HERE SWEET CHILD

A time will never come when God can't change the circumstances in our lives. When things are at their worst, when we are absolutely helpless, God reaches down with his strong hand to pull us up from the depths of despair!

Allowing fear to control my thoughts, I fretted all night. Just before sunrise I slipped from the bed to find a place of solace. I stepped into the shower, and turned the water on full blast to muffle the sound of my cry to heaven. "Oh God, please spare Kim! Don't leave her in this state! Lord, if she cannot be healed, please let her know I am here. I can't bear the thought of Kim dying without knowing I arrived!"

As the warm spirit of Jesus wrapped around me, the words, "Everything is all right," permeated my soul. The Lord of Lords understood my plea.

Dan and I returned to the hospital in time for morning visitation hours. We hoped for an overnight miracle, but our expectations dimmed when we walked into Intensive Care. Kim appeared less agitated. She no longer thrashed about on the bed, and her lips were free of the echoing "Uh-uh", but Kim's stillness did nothing to allay our fears. She lay staring to the right as she had the day before, and if our daughter knew when we entered the room, she made no sign to prove it.

A gauze pad and large bandage covered Kim's right eye. The attending nurse informed us, "Her eyes have crossed because of the increased intracranial pressure. Doctor Carlton left orders for us to alternate a patch on one eye each day to relieve the eye strain. Don't worry. her eyes will return to normal over time."

Yearning to penetrate Kim's strange wall of silence, I leaned over her bed. "Kimmie, it's Mom. Daddy and I are here. How's my sweet little girl today?"

Silence, along with a continued stare in the opposite direction from me, served as her reply.

I willed myself to resist the urge to sweep her up into my arms and run to safety—a place where I could hold her and protect her from the hands of death. Woefully, no such place existed, and my body remained too weak to lift her.

I pointed toward a chair across the room. "Dan, would you please carry Kim over there so I can hold her?"

His frown deepened the lines on his forehead. "No. I'm afraid to move her. She doesn't have any motor control, and the muscles in her neck are too weak. I don't want to take a chance on hurting her."

As if in answer to my plea, the nurse returned to check Kim's vital signs. After making notations on the chart, she looked up and asked, "Mrs. Grissom would you like to hold Kim?"

The tears dripping from my eyes signaled my response.

The RN immediately gathered extra pillows while instructing me to sit in the chair. The moment I sat down, she pushed and tucked pillows around me, then added extra ones on my left side to properly support Kim's head.

"Now we're ready for Kim," she announced.

With great care and expertise, the woman clad in white

lifted our child from the bed and carried her to my outstretched arms. When Kim was properly settled, Dan and the nurse slipped quietly from the room.

Peace descended upon my soul. My arms held Kimmie for the first time in eight, long days. I treasured each second of our time together while feeling the warmth of her tiny body close to mine. Fearing this love flowing between my child and me might one day be gone forever, I clutched her tightly. Kim's eyes continued to stare fixedly in the same direction.

Does she know I am here?

I gently placed my hand under her head and neck, then carefully turned her face toward me. "Kim, it's Mom. I am here Kimmie; everything is all right."

I repeated these same words countless times, but she never reacted to my voice. I forged on through the silence. I needed to reach my child!

"Kim, it's Mom. I'm here Kimmie."

At last came the soft whisper I longed to hear, *"Okay."*

My heart exploded! With relief flooding my being, I spoke the same words again while adding, "Just close your eyes honey, and go to sleep; everything will be all right."

"Okay."

I breathed a sigh of relief. "Thank you Lord for giving me proof she can hear!"

Within seconds, Kim's eyes closed in sleep, and her taunt body relaxed in my arms.

One hour later, the same nurse returned to check Kim's vital signs, and stated, "We need to get her back into bed."

At the very moment the nurse lifted her from my arms, Kim's one unfettered eye sprang open. Oh Kimmie, you did know whose arms were holding you!

After the nurse withdrew from the room, I walked to Kim's

bed, and stood beside her speaking incessantly so she would be aware of my presence. When I could no longer stand, I sat in the chair adjacent to her bed. I wanted her to be certain I had not left the room, so I began to sing her favorite lullabies.

Kim lay on the bed without moving. Her head was turned away from me with the one visible eye peering toward the curtained glass wall. My throat became hoarse, so I stopped singing. When my voice went silent, Kim's head pivoted, and her eye rotated in my direction for a mere second.

I jumped to my feet. "Thank you, Father! Now I am certain she is aware of voices and her surroundings, but for some unknown reason she can't communicate with us."

Chapter 14 - Mysterious Shadows

Just before dusk, Dan's parents and sister drove into town for a visit. We stood around Kim's bed searching for reasons to explain her silence.

Mary commented on Kim's new facial expression. "Look! Kimmie's got a little pout on her face."

She touched her husband's shoulder. "J.D., you know that look. Every time you teased Kim, she rolled her eyes and puckered her lips pretending to be annoyed."

"Maybe Kim's mad at everybody," J.D. replied. "I can't blame her. This sweet baby has been through too much. They just keep poking and prodding her."

I blamed myself. Kim was hurled into the most terrifying ordeal of her life, and the one person whom she depended upon the most, failed her. Numerous tests, painful injections, and countless strangers took their toll upon her. I was not present to shield and comfort her. I believed Kim waited for me as long as she could before retreating into another world of her own … a place where she could ignore everyone and everything.

When visiting hours were over, we involuntarily said goodbye to Kim and drove to Gary and Beth's home. I didn't want to leave. If what I believed proved true, then my deserting her overnight might inflict further injury upon Kim. Once more, I began to believe in myself. *I caused her illness.* It's easy to believe anything if you want it badly enough, but life did not permit me to bask in my theory for long.

At 11:05 p.m., the phone rang. Within seconds, Gary summoned Dan. Our hearts began to pound violently. A phone call this late at night could only come from one source.

"Hello," Dan said cautiously. "Yes." ... "Okay." ... "I'll be right there." He hung up the phone and quickly reached for his jacket. From the corner of his eye, he saw me standing nearby waiting for the news.

"Babe, everything's okay. Don't get upset—"

"What's going on?" I demanded.

"A nurse noticed Kim couldn't move the left side of her body, so she called Dr. Carlton. He's at the hospital now, and wants to run tests and X-rays. She may have a blood clot forming in her brain."

I stood frozen in terror; my throat constricted with a silent scream.

Motioning to his brother, Dan lifted his chin. "You want to go with me to the hospital?" Gary returned a nod of assent and pulled his jacket from the coat closet.

I snapped to attention, "I'll be right back; let me get my coat."

Dan spun toward me with his hand on the doorknob. "You need to stay here and get some rest. You just got out of the hospital, and there isn't anything we'll be able to do except walk the floor. You'll be better off here than in a hospital. I've got to go; the doctor's waiting! I'll call you as soon as I find out anything."

The door slammed behind them, and Beth and I were left to stare at one another. I scuttled to the bedroom where I allowed my tears to flow with abandon. Beth followed, sat beside me on the bed, and wept. Her tears were strangely comforting.

No one had ever cried with me before. We bowed our heads in prayer, but neither of us knew what to say. I wanted Kim's life spared, yet I didn't want her to suffer any more. We could only ask God to take care of her.

On impulse, shortly after midnight, I phoned my parents. A call at such a late hour would terrify them, but I couldn't help myself. My world was crashing around me, and like a frightened child, I turned to my parents for shelter from the terrible storm.

Although God had answered each of my prayers, I remained unable to grasp the concept of total trust. I possessed the faith to make my requests known unto God, yet I lacked the greater faith to simply ASK and BELIEVE. Instead, I reached for the phone and sought solace from my parents.

Dan and Gary returned around three in the morning. In one frightening moment, just before the two walked through the door, a horrible thought flashed through my mind. Their faces revealed nothing when they walked in.

Panicking, I screamed, "Is she dead?"

At first Dan stood in shock; then he pulled me into his arms. "No, no, she's okay! The doctor just ran tests to make sure Kim hasn't developed a blood clot. He didn't find anything."

Relieved, I questioned him further, but he couldn't offer much information. "They didn't find anything new. Dr. Carlton is going to stay at the hospital and recheck every test and X-ray to make sure he hasn't overlooked anything. He sent Gary and me home to get some rest. One thing's for sure, the doctor's doing everything he can to help Kim."

"Yes," I answered. "We're blessed to have someone who's willing to spend all night looking for answers."

With sudden alarm, I remembered my parents. They must

still be waiting for news! I made a brief call to reassure them before going to bed.

We rose early, having had less than four hours of rest, and were just beginning to dress when the phone rang. The hospital's ICU supervisor called requesting to speak with Dan.

"Dr. Carlton wants to send Kim for more air studies and tests," she informed. "We need your written consent as soon as possible."

I threw my makeup and brush in my purse. We grabbed our coats, and sped to the hospital. We were certain the doctor suspected something serious to call before seven o'clock in the morning after staying up the greater part of the night.

Hour upon hour trudged wearily by. Dan paced; I worried. We heard a rustling sound from the hallway just before a haze of green uniform charged into the room.

Doctor Carlton spoke expeditiously. "I know nothing definite yet, but I found a blockage at the base of the skull."

Before we could utter one word, he spun around and sprinted back to X-ray.

Dan and I stared at one another. What does that mean? We were condemned to wait for three more hours before we could ascertain anything.

At approximately four in the afternoon, the doctor returned; this time he sat down in a chair adjacent to us. Dr. Carlton found the blockage he spoke of earlier, but he also discovered something new in the X-rays.

"I found a tiny spot in the very center of her brain. It is impossible with X-rays to determine exactly what the shadow is. I'm sorry, but only symptoms, and time, can determine what the spot might be. An exploratory surgery could well take her life; we have no other choice."

Whether we simply could not comprehend what the physician said, or we just did not want to believe it, I can't say. I only know Dan and I lived in limbo. For us, nothing had changed. Kim's condition remained the same, and no one knew the cause or cure for it. Some unknown shadow controlled the actions in this drama, and we were incapable of stopping it.

I, in particular, could not accept the doctor's implication concerning the shadow in the X-ray. I chose to ignore the facts. It was easier to believe Kim had retreated into a world where no one could ever harm her again.

Looking back, my reasoning sounds absurd, but at times, the mind tunes out all reason and focuses instead on its own desires.

Dan never tried to dissuade me; he simply held my hand instead of breaking my heart further with the truth. I chose to believe the only prescription she needed was love, and if ever a child could be surrounded and healed with love, it was Kim. The heart holds sway over the mind, denying it the ability to accept the unacceptable.

The following morning, Dr. Carlton unequivocally brought me out of my fantasy and planted me firmly into stark reality. Dan and I were standing on opposite sides of Kim's bed when he walked in flanked by a nurse, the charge nurse, and the ward supervisor. Before the doctor could speak, I plunged past my embarrassment to ask a question which was certain to be deemed ludicrous. I needed to know the answer.

"Dr. Carlton, is it possible Kim's problem could be psychological?" He began to shake his head, but I doggedly continued, "After all, she has never had an experience such as this, and for me to be gone—"

Dr. Carlton interrupted my query with blunt words aimed to slice through my delusional thinking with the precision of a knife. "There is a physical reason for Kim's illness. The spot we found in the X-ray definitely exists. It most likely is either a tumor or a blood clot. In both instances it could possibly mean death."

I lowered my head in an attempt to shield myself from the egregious barrage of words, but the doctor forged his way past my armor.

"If it is a tumor, whether benign or malignant, it means certain death. It is located in the very center of the brain, and there is absolutely nothing we can do. We could operate and perhaps scrape away some of the tumor, but it would most likely cause death or leave her virtually helpless the rest of her life.

"If it is a blood clot, it could simply take care of itself, but the chances of the clot causing her death are much greater."

I pulled my shoulders forward, and folded my arms across my body to deflect the awful truth. I couldn't bear to hear another word, but amid the droning cacophony of doom, a snippet of hope penetrated the air. My head jerked upward in rapt attention as my heart latched on to Dr. Carlton's last sentence.

"On the other hand, Kim might suddenly snap out of this, and we might never know what has happened to her."

Oh yes! These were the words I wanted to hear; these were words I could believe. But I would never wonder what happened. I'd know with certainty God answered our prayers.

Instantly, we realized no one else put much faith in the doctor's last remark. The room rapidly became a revolving door filtering a constant stream of nurses and various officials. First, Kim's nurse returned and pushed a chair next to the bed. "I'll bring Kim to you so you can hold her."

Our child's nourishment now depended solely upon intravenous fluids. With amazing speed and gentleness the nurse lifted Kimmie from the bed and placed her in my lap without disturbing the delicate tube or needle. I held Kim in my arms while fiercely fighting back the screams bubbling up inside of me.

Precipitously, the supervisor reappeared. She spoke a few words of comfort just before delivering the mortal blow. "Mr. and Mrs. Grissom, because Kim is so young, and because we do not know how much more time you will have with her, the rules regarding your visits to intensive care have been changed. Both of you may stay with her as much as you want throughout the day."

Moments after the supervisor quietly left the room, another woman pushed her way through the doorway. She introduced herself as a social worker and offered to help us with any "*possible arrangements.*"

Dan and I stared at one other in shocked silence. What is happening? Has everyone suddenly given up? Does everyone believe Kim is on her death bed?

No, not everyone has given up. Somehow, someway, Kim is going to live! I will *not* let her die! In my wildest imaginings I could never visualize life without her. Many others in the world may have lost a child, but I could not be one of them.

With the nurse's assistance, I laid Kim back upon the bed. Dan and I were devastated. We needed time to process the various thoughts bouncing around in our heads. We reached for each other's hand and walked in silence down the long, white corridor and through the huge metal doorway ushering us into another world.

Outside the walls of ICU, people scurried by as though nothing had changed. We needed to get away from the happy faces of families taking their loved ones home, and away from the bright smiles of nurses.

Dan suggested a walk outside to get some fresh air. I vaguely remember the walk; my eyes were too blinded by tears to see anything clearly. We stumbled to the car where we could be alone. The second the doors were closed, we were in each other's arms—crying for Kim and for ourselves.

Our tears temporarily released the pent up anguish in our hearts and enabled us to at last speak. I assume our first reaction was only natural. We needed to find a reason for the devastation being thrust upon our lives, and the blame must fall squarely upon our shoulders. Kim's sweet innocence certainly could not be held accountable for any wrong doing; the cause must be something in our lives.

We searched our innermost secrets. Neither of us led exemplary lives. We were both Christians, yet we failed to live up to the responsibilities inherent with our salvation. I couldn't remember the last time I had told someone about Jesus. I still prayed, but not with the close affinity to God I once enjoyed. Admittedly, I fell into step with so many others my age wherein I placed my family and home before God. Little time was left in the day for meditation and a talk with my Savior; the beds must be made, meals must be prepared, and dishes needed to be washed.

Dan shared my feelings of guilt as well. Both of us knew for certain we had failed in our Christian lives. Now we believed God was reaching out to us, and using Kim as his rod of correction.

In the parking lot of the hospital, we bowed our heads and prayed, "Lord, if Kim is suffering for our sins, please forgive us. Lead us in a new direction and remove this affliction from our child."

In the aftermath of our prayer, calm prevailed, but things were not settled in my heart. I yearned to get down on my knees in continuous prayer until the whole matter was resolved. My prayer remained unanswered, and I didn't know God's will concerning Kim.

A very dear person of faith has since defined fasting as not only the giving up of food, but also the giving up of everything in our lives while we hunger and thirst for God's presence, and seek answers for our trials.

My personal quest to receive a reply from God began on this morning. I knocked on his door continuously. Often there were times of tears and loud outcries for God to help Kim. "Either take her home or heal her, but in any case, remove her from the indeterminate state in which she exists!"

At other times I shed tears of regret for my past sins while asking God to forgive me. "Lord, tell me what you want me to do. I am willing to do anything if my sins are the reason for all this heartache!"

I wailed and moaned for his divine mercy. Yet I did not receive the answer I sought. My prayers, and the groaning of my soul, persisted for weeks as I held onto God while seeking an answer. When fears assaulted me from every direction, I cried aloud, "God, are you even listening to me?" At times I felt as though the wall I had built through the years of indifference to God's service made it impossible for me to penetrate heaven's portal.

My heavenly Father did not answer my prayer quickly, but neither did he forsake me. God's silence was never about what I could do, or what I promised to do. We can promise God anything in the midst of turmoil, but our human weaknesses will never allow us to be the perfect person we promise to be.

Although at times I felt alone and out of touch with God, his love and strength were never withdrawn.

> *"For the Lord will not cast off for ever: But though he cause grief, yet will he have compassion according to the multitude of his mercies. For he doth not afflict willingly nor grieve the children of men" (Lam. 3:31–33).*

CHAPTER 15 - DARE I SUBMIT?

Days passed with little change in Kim's condition. Standing watch beside her, I vigilantly sought any hint of improvement—either in a movement, or a flicker in her eyes—but no glimmer of her former self ever appeared. Aside from the day when she whispered the word *"Okay,"* Kim never responded to anything I did or said. I was thoroughly confused and often resentful.

What does God want from me? I've asked for his forgiveness, and promised him a new life. I've repeatedly begged for his mercy upon Kim, yet nothing has changed!

I don't know how many times I tripped over these same thoughts. I became self-righteous and bitter. All of these things are happening because of me! My life and my failures caused Kim's illness!

Truly the Lord acts swiftly to correct us when we stray. He desires to lead us back onto the right path, and away from the briars of life where we often roam; but God's plan was more elaborate than I could have ever imagined.

He didn't allow Kim's illness in order to punish one lowly mother; instead, God intended for countless lives to be touched and turned toward a new direction in Christ.

Nevertheless, before my Father could use me, he must first humble me. He stripped me of my pride by showing me just how little I could do to help my child. Neither my love, or attention, nor any rash promises of change in my life, could bring about Kim's recovery.

On Sunday night, the third day of March, Dan said goodbye with a heavy heart. The time arrived for us to switch roles. He drove home to return to work and to help care for our other two children, and I assumed the role of Kim's lone caregiver.

Alone, with only my bitter thoughts to keep me company, I wrestled with God all night. By daybreak, I understood what I must do. When I arrived at the hospital on Monday morning, I walked to the hospital chapel and knelt behind the last pew.

I bowed my head, but I could not bring myself to utter the words I needed to say. The battle within my soul raged relentlessly. How could I yield my will to God? His thoughts about Kim might not be the same as mine. What if God said, "No?" My heart warred against my stubborn will. I wanted things to be as they were. I wanted my child back!

"Dear God, I can't speak the words I know you want me to say. I just can't!"

God's spirit wrapped itself around me. His presence became palpable. "Let go child; let go."

I recalled the image of my child lying eerily still; the struggle within my heart ceased when I realized Kim's well-being far outweighed my needs. My selfishness held her hostage in an abyss of nothingness.

With tears streaming from my eyes, I cried, "Lord, Kim is yours. You alone know what is best for all our lives. She was your child long before she was mine; so now Father, I give her to you. Let not my will, but *your* will be done."

Those few sentences were the most difficult words to ever pass from my lips. Kim was God's child. "Know ye that the Lord he is God: it is he that hath made us, and not we ourselves; we are his people, and the sheep of his pasture" (Ps. 100:3). Kim came from my body, but only as a blessed gift from heaven. I had no claims upon her.

Immediately following my prayer of total submission, God's love began to manifest itself in discernable ways. We saw no hint of Kim's awareness of the world around her for four long days, but within hours of my prayer, hope resurfaced.

A nurse came to administer Kim's medication. The instant the needle touched her flesh, Kim's leg flinched. At first, I was stunned by what I witnessed. *She reacted to pain!* Joy filled my being, yet shame consumed me because I rejoiced in my child's anguish.

Kim's reaction to pain was our first signal she might be waking from what the doctor medically labeled a stupor. Although this response was encouraging, no one could ascertain whether Kim heard voices or understood our words, but events on Tuesday morning offered me renewed optimism.

A nurse entered the room carrying a tray of instruments just before Dr. Carlton bustled through the doorway. He paused momentarily to address me. "I've come to remove the bandages and sutures from Kim's incision."

At first I planned to remain in the room, but thinking better of it, I decided to wait in the lobby. Within fifteen minutes, I observed Dr. Carlton emerge from ICU and walk to the elevator, so I slipped quietly back into the room. Kim lay on her side, facing the door. I began my customary one-sided dialogue as I stepped toward her, but midway across the room, my feet stopped their forward motion. My voice went silent. Pity for my helpless daughter overwhelmed me; the urge to sympathize gained control.

"Have they hurt my Kimmie again?"

Instantly, Kim's eyes clouded with tears. Her mouth drooped in a pout; her face became blotched with speckles of red. *Kim heard me!* More importantly, she understood me, and her precious little soul wanted to cry in response.

Joy overwhelmed me, but my elation lasted mere seconds before I realized the horrible circumstances in which my child existed. Her mind and soul remained vital, but they were locked inside a body unable to move, a voice unable to speak, and eyes unable to cry.

A sick, agonizing feeling swept my soul. I attempted to place myself in the position of my bright, energetic daughter. I tried to imagine what it must be like to think, to want to speak, and yet not be able to utter my thoughts. As an adult, I could not begin to understand such a situation. How could a two-year-old child cope with having no voice and no ability to escape an unfathomable prison?

Dear God, please help me console my child! I carefully lifted Kim from the bed and carried her to a nearby chair where I held her until she fell asleep. She could not speak or move, but I was positive she could feel my arms around her and the love pouring from my heart. I believed she received comfort from my touch.

With the exception of a budding alertness, Kim's condition essentially remained the same. Her frail body began to tremble whenever she sensed someone new walking into the room. Everyone, including the nurses, attributed it to acute nervousness and anxiety. The left side of her body remained immobile, while her right arm and leg batted endlessly against the bed on which she lay.

On Wednesday, Dr. Carlton began an all-out effort to stabilize Kim's condition, and rebuild her emaciated body. Following his orders, nurses removed the insidious looking eye patch, and inserted a nasal-gastric tube into her nose, and threaded it down into her stomach through the esophagus. This tube made it possible to feed her a high protein supplement, along with water, every two hours. Within a few short days, Kim's legs were once again round and firm. Her abdomen, which had sunk beneath the jutting pelvic bone, was once again rounding out, and her vital signs were improving rapidly.

Increasingly stronger body tremors became the only noticeable deterrent to her improved health. I never thought about the tremors being anything more than simple fright. Each time a doctor, nurse, or visitor walked into the room, Kim's tremors visibly increased, thus confirming my assumption. When I mentioned my latest observation to the doctor, he could only offer me the hope of a quieter room once she was able to leave intensive care.

Friday morning my pastor and I were visiting in the ICU waiting room when Doctor Carlton exited the circular nursing station and walked toward us. The doctor allowed himself a faint smile. "Kim's vital signs have stabilized. Her condition has improved enough for us to safely transfer her to the pediatric wing. I'm assigning her to a room where she can receive continuous monitoring. The nurses are preparing for her immediate transfer."

My heart exploded with gratitude. The time was long overdue for me to express my appreciation for his concern and dedication toward the improved health of our daughter. As the words tumbled out, I watched the doctor's countenance take on a tenderhearted demeanor while his eyes clouded.

Dr. Carton briefly averted his eyes before answering, "I wish I could do more."

Without further words, he turned and briskly walked away while I stood in stunned surprise. This brusque, decisive man, who saw death and suffering every day, had undoubtedly been touched by our little Kim. Compassion lay beneath his dense veneer of professionalism.

The visit with my pastor ended shortly afterward, and I returned to Kim and helped with the necessary preparations for her transfer. I gathered up her many gifts and cards, then began my farewell to each of her kind and caring nurses. Part of me feared leaving the security of the Intensive Care Unit, but joy outweighed any concerns. At last I could spend the night with Kim. There would be no more long nights wondering whether she was awake and asking for me—no more wondering about her condition. This move must mean Kim was getting better. She appeared more responsive, healthier looking, and stabilized.

CHAPTER 16 - A BRIGHT WORLD BECOMES FOREBODING DARKNESS

I stood in a bright new world. Kim and I were no longer residents of a cylindrical bubble of glass walls looking directly into the rooms of other critically ill patients. While Kim rested from her transfer to Pediatrics, I surveyed our new surroundings. I could easily imagine this room becoming a soothing oasis for a traumatized little girl.

The room gave us ample space, and included a fold-out bed for me, a closet, and an adjoining half-bath. Most importantly, solid walls separated us from other patients. An oddly placed window was centered in the wall to the right of the entry door. Although such a large window offered us less privacy from on-lookers entering or exiting the hallway, nothing could really dampen my spirit. No one could force me to leave Kim tonight.

Four shelves stretched across the length of the east side of the room below a bank of glistening windows. The top wooden ledge provided the perfect place for Kim's vast array of gifts and stuffed animals. A huge, three-foot rabbit with gigantic ears, took up one half of the space. Nestled to the right of the rabbit, I placed smaller versions of bunnies, bears, and puppies to stand watch. The second shelf conveniently housed Kim's beautiful gowns with room to spare.

I held the brown velvet dachshund with its perky little grey and yellow cap. This tiny creature with its large eyes and sweet, hand-sewn smile, deserved a special place. It was responsible for giving Kim courage and comfort through all the preceding days of pain and suffering. I bestowed a quick kiss upon one of "Missy Dog's" floppy ears just before placing it on the bed within easy reach of Kim's hand. Lastly, I shelved each of the books I packed on the day the baby and I were released from the hospital. Their illustrated pages served as a reminder of happier times.

Before our tiny cosmos crumbled, the children ran to me multiple times each day bearing arm loads of books, while pleading, "Mom, let's read!"

Dirk took his place in the rocking chair just to my right while I lifted Kim onto my lap. Whenever I tried to hurry things along by skipping over parts of the story, one of the children called my attention to it. "Member Mom, you forgot ... ."

I believed these same books held restorative power and a return to normalcy. When I couldn't think of any more comforting words or phrases, I reached for those books to fill the void. I hoped the words from their pages might reconnect Kim with her family.

By noon, each of the pediatric nurses had welcomed us, and Kim and I were settled in our new home. I began to feel more at ease, but Kim's tremors were rapidly increasing. Because no one else exhibited concern about the tremors, I surmised our sudden change to new surroundings contributed to her anxiety.

I could properly support and hold Kim by this time, so I took her for a walk around the room. I carried her to the row of windows overlooking the busy street below. After weeks of seeing nothing other than curtains and glass walls, Kimmie received her first glimpse of the outside world. "Look honey, can you feel the warm sunshine coming in? Doesn't it feel good?

Now I can bring you over to feel the sun, or to watch all the cars speeding by, anytime you want."

I walked over to a green-leather rocking chair located within easy reach of her books, and sat down while gently cradling my daughter. I held Kim throughout the following hours, rocking her, singing lullabies, and holding her trembling hands.

Shortly after three-thirty in the afternoon, Kim seemed calm enough for me to leave a few moments to get something to drink. Determined to be gone only a short time, I raced down the stairs to the coffee shop, but when I returned fifteen minutes later, Kim's skin burned bright red with fever. I touched her forehead; heat seared beneath my hand.

I bolted toward the nurses' station directly across the hall to summon help. The nurse on duty reported, "Her temperature has just been checked, and medication is on its way."

Twenty minutes following the administering of the medication, Kim's body sizzled with fever. I watched her skin color advance from rose to a dark shade of crimson. In seconds, she appeared severely burned. I ran to the nurses' station. Every available nurse had been summoned to assist with an emergency down the hall.

Panicking, I sped back to Kim and grabbed washcloths and cold water to cool her skin. Moments later, the fever spiked, and Kim's body began to tremble incessantly. I needed to get help, yet I feared leaving my child. Just as I turned toward the nurses' station, Beth appeared at the door. I hurriedly asked her to stay with Kim while I searched for a nurse.

I trotted up and down the hall until I found a nursing assistant who promised to send someone as soon as possible. I ran back to the room only to find Kim in violent seizures. Suddenly her head jerked backward, and her back arched to such an extent it raised her body from the bed, then she began to vomit.

I charged toward the door, and almost crashed into a nurse entering the room with another injection. With rapid strides the LVN assessed the situation, rolled Kim onto her left side to prevent any choking, and instructed an aide to change the linens. The crisis reached its climax, and Kim's fever broke. When her stomach expelled its contents, her body relaxed, and she fell asleep.

Kim slept in my arms while the linens were changed; she didn't rouse when I placed her back on the bed. She slept peacefully throughout the remainder of the afternoon and into the evening. Her eyes never opened throughout the hourly monitoring of vital signs, nor during her feedings. Great relief pulsated through me when I witnessed her resting so well. Throughout the previous thirteen days, Kim slept only in brief intervals. Today's crisis became our turning point. I made my nightly call to Dan with a light heart.

"Honey, things were kind of scary this afternoon. Kim's temperature climbed out of control, and she began having seizures. But then her fever broke, and she fell asleep. She's been sleeping ever since. I think she's finally getting the rest she needs. Her tremors have stopped too. Maybe it won't be long now before we can come home."

Thanking God with each step, I returned to the room. For the first time since my arrival, I could spend the night with Kim.

At around ten o'clock, the alarm bells began striking one by one in my head. It's been six hours since Kim fell asleep. She's slept through vital signs, neuro checks, feedings, and injections. I once again checked the humiliating diaper she must detest wearing. It was still dry. Something is very wrong! She's had three feedings since the last time I changed her!

The charge nurse stepped in briefly to check on Kim. I spoke with her about my fears. "She's slept too long without stirring, and her diaper is still dry after six hours."

The nurse failed to be overly concerned; she simply took a mental note of my observations, and nodded her head once in my direction before leaving the room.

Could I be overreacting? I decided to wait a little longer before becoming too alarmed. One hour later, Kim slept soundly, and her diaper remained dry. I patted her hand while speaking her name ... softly at first ... then more forcefully. "Kim? Kimmie Dawn!" I couldn't get a response.

At eleven o'clock, a new nursing shift began, so I again stepped across the hall and relayed my fears to the new Registered Nurse in charge. She immediately marched back to the room with me, and made every effort to awaken Kim without receiving a response.

Looking at me from across the bed, the nurse explained, "Mrs. Grissom, there's no mention of this on Kim's chart by the previous nursing staff. I'm sorry, but I must observe Kim myself and compile sufficient notation before I can report her condition to the doctor."

Throughout the following hour, the nurse periodically returned, and attempted to rouse Kim. Between intervals, I sat at Kim's bedside pleading with her to wake up. Shortly after midnight, the nurse informed me she had completed her observation. "I'm ready to call the doctor."

Within moments, she returned. Speaking softly, and with compassion, she stated, "Dr. Carlton has confirmed my assessment of Kim. All bladder function has now ceased. He has given the necessary orders to insert a *Foley*."

She had no need to say anything further. No one expected Kim to wake up.

I paced the hall fighting the urge to phone Dan, and with new resolve, turned to God instead. I walked to the alcove of the stairwell, and in the quiet solitude above those descending steps, I pleaded with God to have mercy on Kim, and to give me the strength to withstand the things to come.

The following hours will be forever etched in my memory. Loneliness and utter despair attacked my soul. Kim was slipping away from me, and I could do nothing to stop her descent. Yet God never leaves us without comfort. His children are everywhere, and He purposefully sends them where and when they are needed.

While I sat beside Kim fighting tears, the same nurse who had just confirmed my worst fears, slipped back into the room. For the first time, I noticed the name, "Pam," on her identification tag. She wore white knit pants, a loose fitting blouse, and comfortable sneakers instead of the standard white starched dress and one-inch heels. Additionally, her short, russet curls were not confined beneath a traditional white cap.

The nurse's casual attire and soft-spoken words put me at ease. She assured, "God will provide all the strength you need."

Leaving only for brief periods to tend her other duties, Pam sat with me throughout most of her shift. Her presence helped me survive the long, tortuous night. She listened wordlessly while I poured my heart out. When I purged my soul of every expression of grief, she spoke for the first time. "She's in God's hands. He'll take care of her."

Shortly after five o'clock in the morning, she convinced me to call Dan. "He has a right to know, and you need his support as well."

The only phone available before six o'clock in the morning

was located downstairs in the Surgical Waiting Room. A woman and two men, were sitting in the room when I closed the door to the phone booth.

I heard the fear in Dan's voice when he accepted the collect call from the operator. He didn't wait for a "Hello," but instead blurted, "What's wrong?"

Reining in my fears, I calmly explained, step by step, every event of the night. I thought he understood my meaning, but Dan had the same problem as I. He didn't want to believe the truth.

"Now, just stay calm," he soothed. "Everything is going to be all right. I'll be there as soon as I can after work today and—"

"Dan! Don't you understand? Our little girl is dying!"

The dam burst for both of us as the words I had been too afraid to think, much less express, came tumbling out. A stunned silence hung in the air between us before I heard a gut-wrenching sob and the cry, "Oh, no!"

We each stood crying into the phones. No words could penetrate the grief. Following a lengthy sigh, Dan murmured, "I'll be there as soon as I can."

Unable to speak, we silently hung up. I exhaled a shuddering breath, stepped from the booth, and fell into the arms of the woman who had been sitting in the waiting room. She overheard my conversation, and when I opened the door of the booth, she sprang up from her chair to embrace me.

As though it had been pre-planned, the woman lived in my hometown. Her uncle was undergoing emergency heart surgery at this same hour. Amid her own crisis, she took the time to comfort me, and to offer a prayer. God's grace surrounded me.

I mechanically plodded my way back up the two flights of stairs to the pediatric floor. With my hope having vanished, I didn't expect any changes when I walked through the door. The nurse sat vigilantly beside Kim. I leaned over the bed rail and stood staring at my daughter. Kim's countenance exuded blissful peace. Perhaps this was the reason I could not reach her. Had Kim's spirit stealthily escaped from her fast failing body? Was she standing outside heaven's gate?

Pam kept watch with me throughout the following two hours—well past the end of her shift. She sat beside Kim when Dan suddenly appeared at the door. An awkward moment ensued. My husband and I neither spoke nor moved toward one another. Wrapped in our sorrow, and glued to the floor, we both looked down upon the child we so dearly loved.

The nurse slipped silently away, and shortly afterward, Dad entered the room. Tears streamed from his weary and saddened eyes while he beheld our sleeping angel. Our tongues failed us. The grief was too great to express.

The clock struck seven o'clock in the morning; the three of us could do nothing other than wait for the doctor's arrival to confirm our greatest fear. Dan and Dad anxiously paced the floor while I sat beside Kim. My heart overflowed with so many things I wanted to say. I had a lifetime of words and wishes surging through my heart and perhaps mere moments to express them.

"Kimmie, I love you so much. I've loved you from the first moment I saw you. You were so beautiful, and my heart just melted the first time I saw those big, blue eyes. I couldn't wait to bring you home so I could hold and cuddle you all the time.

"Dirk was excited to meet you too. As soon as we brought you home from the hospital, he climbed onto the couch and held out his hands so I could place you in his arms. He loves you so much, and he asks about you every day.

"You have always been Daddy's little girl, and he would do anything for you. Kimmie, Daddy is here with us right now. He came today because he loves you with all his heart. Pawpaw is here too. He and Granny love you very much."

Leaning across the locked bed rail, I kissed Kim's cheek before continuing my goodbye. "Honey, when you were just a tiny little baby, you slept in a pretty yellow bassinet in Mommy and Daddy's room. I just wanted to be able to hear you breathe so I would know you were safe, and now I want the very same thing for you Kimmie. I want to hold you close to me and keep you safe. I love you from the tip of your nose to the tip of your toes, now and forever.

"Always remember this Kimmie: "Daddy, Mommy, and Dirk love you. And you know what, Kim? Granny and Pawpaw, and Grandma and Grandpa, love you too. Hold on, Sweetie; hold on."

Time had no meaning amid the endless pacing and silence. One of the nurses offered to sit with Kim while we went for coffee. "If the doctor arrives before you get back, I'll have you paged."

Reluctantly, the three of us walked down to the coffee shop and ordered. Just as we sat down, our names were called over the intercom. We flew upstairs with our heads and hearts throbbing.

Dr. Carlton stood beside Kim completing his examination. Deliberately avoiding my eyes, he looked directly toward Dan.

"Your daughter has had a bad night. She is comatose, and I think now we can assume she does have a cancerous tumor. Death is inevitable, and there is nothing further we can do. I'm very sorry."

Dan clutched me in his arms while I openly wept. His right hand reached up to caress my cheek and draw me closer to him in an unconscious attempt to shield me from the world. A nurse pulled me away and seated me in a nearby chair so the doctor could speak privately with Dan and Dad in the hallway. I wanted to slide down from the chair onto the floor and simply melt into oblivion, but the nurse placed her hand on my shoulder and said, "God is with you. He will not desert you."

Why was the doctor's report such a shock? I had lived with the reality of Kim's death since midnight. But hope never dims until we are faced with stark reality. I sank into a dark hole. Everything went black, and I lacked the will to pull myself out of the darkness.

"Babe, are you okay?"

Dan's voice penetrated my wall of despair. I slowly shifted toward the sound. He knelt on the floor beside my chair; his steel-blue eyes connected with mine and pulled me from the morass. His hand drew my head toward his shoulder. "Are you all right?"

I blinked back tears. "No, I'm not sure that will ever be possible again, but I'm glad you're here."

I turned my attention toward the bed. Dad gently stroked Kim's right hand while speaking the words, "Most Gracious Heavenly Father. Blessed Heavenly Father ..."

Smiling through the tears, I watched Daddy pray for Kimmie. Mother was a woman of few words who unwaveringly offered me quiet strength, but for as long as I could remember, Daddy prayed daily with tears streaming from his eyes. He became my tender-hearted anchor in every crisis. Following his prayer, he drove home to relay the new information to our families.

"Why don't you two go for a walk?" the nurse inquired. "I'll stay here with Kim."

Dan pulled me from the chair. "Let's go. You need to get some fresh air."

We stepped soundlessly hand in hand through the long corridors and exited the building. Our feet carried us along the meandering pathway of the sidewalk surrounding the grass and trees. Eventually, upon Dan's suggestion, we walked across the parking lot to our car so we could speak privately. I begged him to tell me what Dr. Carlton had said.

He exhaled a shivering breath before answering, "Well, first of all, Dr. Carlton plans to call the best cancer specialists in Texas to find out if there is anything more we can do, but he's been consulting with them all along."

"What about that children's hospital? Everyone thinks it's where we need to take her. Maybe they have better treatments."

Dan shook his head. "It's a dead end too. He's already called them. They'll take Kim, but it still boils down to the location of the tumor. An operation would kill her."

Through heaving sobs, I demanded, "Did the doctor have *anything* good to say?"

"There's *nothing* good about any of this, and there's nothing anybody can do to change it."

I bit my bottom lip and took deep breaths to stem the flood of tears. "Just tell me what Dr. Carlton said. I have to face whatever it is."

"It's not pretty. He said Kim wouldn't live more than two, or at the most, three weeks. Evidently it's a type of tumor that grows fast, because it only took a few weeks for her to lose motor control, and now her bladder can't function. Doc said it will keep growing until all of her bodily functions cease. Eventually the tumor will grow so large that the brain will hemorrhage, and when it starts bleeding, she'll die."

What a horrible way for my child's life to end! Even more horrifying to me was the prospect of having to sit by and watch these things happen while knowing absolutely nothing could be done.

Dan enveloped me in his arms. I leaned my head upon his shoulder. My husband's errant tear trickled down my cheek while we each prayed silently for mercy.

CHAPTER 17 - FAITH TESTED

Grief is unlike any other emotion. The torment it inflicts upon the soul is limitless.

In mere moments, our hopes and dreams were ripped from us, and our hearts began separate journeys—each threaded its way through every conceivable avenue of grief. Dan became stoic and filled with anger; I turned my grief inward. God, why have you deserted me? Why haven't you answered my prayers? Have I done something so egregious you can't forgive me? Punish me, Lord, but don't take out your anger on Kimmie!

Allowing the former seeds of guilt to return and run rampant, I sat wordlessly beside my husband. Wave upon wave of culpability and shame washed over me. I remembered every unkind thought or word, felt the sting of remorse for putting my home and family above God, and shuddered at my inability to live a perfect life of love and commitment to Jesus Christ. I felt abandoned, unloved, and unworthy of God's forgiveness.

I could not, for one moment, contemplate a life without Kim. I screamed aloud, "Why Lord? Why must Kim suffer and die? Everyone we know has healthy and happy children. Why is this happening to us? Don't you love us as much as you do the others? Even if I am unlovable, don't you care about our sweet, precious child?"

Dan exploded, "It isn't you! Kim is dying because of me! It's my fault!"

The trauma perpetrated upon our lives seemed to be met with silence ... or worse yet ... condemnation from above. In the midst of the anguish burrowing deep within my soul, God's love encompassed me. His Spirit brought me back from the depths of despair by whispering God's message from scripture about the essence of his greatest gift to the world:

> *"For God so loved the world, that he gave his only begotten Son, that whosoever believeth in him should not perish, but have everlasting life. For God sent not his Son into the world to condemn the world; but that the world through him might be saved" (John 3:16–17).*

With sudden clarity, I realized none of the cataclysmic events happening in our lives were conceived in retribution. The God who had been with me all my life—the loving Savior who died in my place—was not standing in condemnation of me.

"Dan, we both know Jesus died for our sins. We were forgiven the second we asked Jesus into our hearts. As sweet and loving as Kim is, she can't die because of our sins and weaknesses. Jesus paid the price long ago at Calvary."

He slammed his fist against the steering wheel. "It sure doesn't feel that way right now!"

"Neither of us has been a model Christian, but I also know at this very moment I've never been closer to God. If he just wanted us back in his will, he accomplished that weeks ago. There must be a better reason for Kim's suffering and death than to merely punish us."

Dan nodded in affirmation, then turned his head to stare out the side window. "We all die at some point, and no one ever promised any of us a long life … but … I wish it was me in that bed instead of her. Kim's never done anything to deserve this!"

"The R.N. who sat with us last night is carrying around a lot of guilt too. A few months ago she had a miscarriage. When she and her husband first found out she was pregnant, they were angry because they didn't think they could afford a child. Now Pam believes she lost the baby because in the beginning they didn't want it."

Dan pivoted toward me. "Do you really think God would take her baby because they were worried about money?"

"No, it bothered me when she first told me her story. I didn't want to think about God lying in wait to pounce on each of us for every misguided thought or deed. But here we are—thinking the very same thing—and believing it's our fault Kimmie is dying."

"That's because I know how rotten I am."

"Honey, God knew they were just scared. He knows our hearts too. Even though we aren't the best Christians in the world, He sent Jesus to die for us anyway."

"I guess we're all just a bunch of sinners. Jesus *had* to save us because we sure couldn't do it for ourselves."

We each bowed our heads in voiceless prayer. Mine was a prayer of repentance.

"Lord, forgive me for lashing out. You alone bore the punishment for our sins; your unending grace and love surrounds us. Please help me push away every false thought and doubt, and let me hear your voice instead. The pain in my heart eats at me; my fears constantly attack me. I need you so much, but this anguish stands between us like an impenetrable mountain. Help me Lord; help me!"

"Are you okay?"

The sound of Dan's voice jolted me from my silent soliloquy with Christ. *"What?"* I shrieked.

His hand gently brushed back my hair. His eyes studied mine. "Are you okay?"

I proffered him a shaky smile and an affirmative nod while choking on my tears. Both of us were far from being okay.

"Dan, I just don't understand it. Less than one month ago, our child was pulling on her red patent 'go-go' boots, primping in the mirror, and running into my arms. Now I am told she will be obliterated from my sight. This can't be happening!"

"You've got to find a way to accept this. It's not going away."

"How can I accept it when I can't even imagine it? It's always been easy for me to trust God, but now, it's hard to have faith when God's purpose involves my heart being excised piece by piece! I don't think I have the strength I need to face this."

I leaned my head on Dan's strong shoulder. His throat constricted as he sat stoically mute. Unwittingly, he rubbed his thumb back and forth across my hand until it began to sting. Our heartbeats drummed in the deafening silence.

I breathed in great gulps of air in an attempt to hold back the torrent of tears threatening to fall.

Dan squeezed my hand to signal it was time for us to leave our mobile sanctuary and return to Kim.

I silently offered one more prayer. "Lord, you're the only one who can give us enough courage to step out of this car, and walk through those imposing doors. The threat of the unknown lurks within its walls, and we can't do it alone."

We walked hand in hand toward the massive white facade of the hospital. I clutched Dan's hand firmly before looking upon the daunting four-story building. Thoughts bubbled up inside of me with such force I couldn't contain them.

"This makes me want to climb up on that roof and shout,

'There are no second chances! Make things right with others before it's too late. Don't let a loved one die without telling them about Jesus!' What we're going through is bad enough, but I can't imagine letting another person die without knowing where he will spend eternity. I wish people could somehow understand that death comes without warning, and then it's too late."

Dan drew in a long, shuddering breath before answering. "A few weeks ago, would we have believed anything like this could happen to us? We thought we had the rest of our lives to spend with Kim. People won't understand until it happens to them, and then it's too late. They'll keep on carrying their petty grudges, and not many of us are great at witnessing. One thing's for sure; we all have an appointment to meet the good Lord."

I shook my head in sorrow. "Yes, but God is the only one who holds the appointment book. Many people on this earth will wish they had picked up the phone to tell someone about Jesus, or at the very least, shown kindness and love."

"Kimmie *knows* we love her. She loves us too. It was the first thing we heard every morning, and the last thing we heard every night. We might have a lot of regrets about a bunch of things, but Kim knows she is loved; it's all she ever talked about. There's one other thing we don't have to worry about; we know Kim will be with God."

I squeezed my husband's hand. He was right. We could face the future knowing there would be no regrets, for surely all Kim had ever known in life was love.

When life's heartaches come, our battle against guilt begins. The war is often hard fought and enduring. Guilt creeps in subtlety to taunt us, then subsides to gather its strength, before returning in full force to drown us in its wake. It is Satan, the accuser, who plants these thoughts in our minds, while trying to drive a wedge between us and God at the very time when we need Him the most. We are able to claim victory in this fight against the enemy by holding on to God and resting in the shelter of his arms.

Feelings of guilt and regret are common threads in the process of grief, but we can't allow them to overtake us. God sees and knows every heart. His aim is to nudge us—to keep us on the right path—not to destroy our lives. He wants to plant us so firmly in his love, that when the storms of life come to toss us about, we can stand rooted in Jesus. The catastrophes we suffer are not about punishment, but rather, they are about building such a deep, personal relationship with Jesus Christ that nothing can destroy us.

CHAPTER 18 - WINDOW OF OPPORTUNITY

Amid the heartaches and turmoil of our lives come great blessings if we are wise enough to look upward. When we seek solace in God's grace and place our trust in Him, his plan slowly unfolds like a beautiful spring rose ... one petal at a time.

While Dan and I sat in the car immersing ourselves in sorrow, our Savior prepared hearts, events, and our two-year-old daughter for his intended purposes. We stepped from the bustling hallway into Kim's room and looked upon our sleeping angel. I describe her in this manner because it's truly how she looked. The nurses carefully bathed and dressed her in a pale pink nightgown. She appeared dainty and fragile lying there, but a greater change became blatantly apparent.

I don't possess the ability to paint a mental image of the physical transformation we saw in Kim. Her beauty surpassed any earthly realm. Surely an angel of God reached down to bestow a tiny sprinkle of the beauty of heaven upon our child. From her first day on earth, she presented a portrait of a pretty little girl with blond curls, brilliant blue eyes, and long, silky lashes, but this visual change went well beyond her former physical appearance. Her face glowed with a radiant beauty and an ethereal sweetness. She had no hair; an ugly gauze cap covered her head, and those striking blue eyes were forever closed; nevertheless, her countenance was captivatingly beautiful.

When Dr. Carlton transferred Kim from the Intensive Care Unit, he assigned her to a room designated as Pediatric Intensive Care. A solitary bed was positioned in front of a large glass window which spanned five feet in length and three feet high. Located directly across from the nurses' station, this giant pane gave the medical staff the ability to visually monitor Kim twenty-four hours a day. Her tiny body, from head to foot, was on constant display. Unfortunately, nurses were not the only ones who could view Kim.

Over the course of our stay, visitors walking down the corridor inevitably stopped to furtively peek through the window and peer at our child. Some only glanced discreetly as they passed. Others strolled by several times in an attempt to be as obscure as possible while curiously gazing. Many simply stepped up to the window and stared, while several unabashedly entered our room to make inquiries. A great number stopped at the nurses' station to ask questions. With regard to any of these scenarios, one statement stood out among the rest: "She is so beautiful!"

How marvelous to think that Kim—lying in a coma, with her head bandaged, and tubes trailing from her body—could be so beautiful she drew the outside world to her. It appeared as though God had brushed her with the beauty of heaven in order to fulfill his purpose.

In the beginning, the window was my nemesis. It drew a steady stream of onlookers, curiosity seekers, and staring eyes at the very time I wanted privacy. Even so, God used the window, and the precious child on the other side of the glass, to attract people from every walk of life, thereby opening up opportunities for me to witness.

When I asked God to forgive me for neglecting his work, I made a promise to tell others about Jesus. Now He held me to my promise. My mission did not require travel to other cities or countries; neither was I forced to leave our room. I simply sat beside Kim day after day, and shared with everyone who stopped to gaze, the story of Jesus' love. God supplied the harvest using an intrusive window and Kim's beauty.

But, on this day, as I tried to become accustomed to the shadow of death and the flow of people outside the room, Jesus used this same window to provide for my needs. Dan had momentarily stepped out of the room when an elderly woman hesitantly tapped on the door. Dread gripped me. I didn't want to face another person who insisted upon hearing the details of Kim's illness.

The woman quickly covered the distance from the door to stand beside me. "I'm so sorry to intrude," she said. "I saw this beautiful child from the hallway, and I felt drawn by God to come in and say these words to you: Jesus loves and cares for you and your precious child. He will never leave you. He will carry you in his arms, and hold you close. Don't be afraid; just trust."

After a quick hug, the woman disappeared as quickly as she had come. I could only bow my head in repentance.

"Lord, forgive me for making everything about myself. Our child is the one who is suffering, and I know you love her. Your love radiates from her being. I am certain you are with us, breathing strength, holding Kim, and surrounding her with angels while preparing a place for her. Our hope stands in you, O God, and no other. Kim's future is certain in you, and established long before she was created. You imbued her with your love, and

that love is eternal. Your hands created light, earth, and life. Those same hands will hold Kimmie in the shelter of your arms."

Word quickly spread back home of Kim's condition. By midafternoon, our families were gathered, and several friends had come to offer us support. Dad returned for his second trip in one day, and brought with him my mother and children. I was blessed with the opportunity to hug my son and baby daughter for the first time in days. I fought the urge to cling to them. I could not let Dirk sense my heartache.

Others entered the room with tears welling, and Dan and I found ourselves comforting them. This was not something we knew we were capable of doing; the words just tumbled out because the Holy Spirit led the way.

At five o'clock in the afternoon, a friend and I were walking toward the elevator when I heard someone calling, "Mrs. Grissom! Mrs. Grissom!"

I turned around, and saw Dr. Carlton sprinting toward me.

"Mrs. Grissom, I've just come from a meeting with the radiologist concerning your daughter. After deliberating, we believe it's worth the effort to try radiation therapy on Kim. We can make no promises; it's a long shot, but it's our only recourse at this time. If you agree, her first treatment can begin Monday morning."

A shaky relief flowed throughout my being. Could radiation be our answer, our reprieve from death? Certainly this day brought many Christians to their knees. Nothing is so earth shaking as the news of a child dying from cancer. Before long, we were the recipients of multiple calls and messages informing us of the prayers being offered for Kim. Therein we received our strength.

Dan and I spent the remainder of the weekend adjusting to the ever present calamity facing us. Each sigh, each irregularity in Kim's breathing, brought us quickly to our feet and to her side. Our hearts quaked with terror when an inhalation was slow in coming.

Each time I pleaded with God, "Please Lord, don't take her—not now Lord—just a little while longer."

I was not ready to give God what I had promised Him. I am so very thankful for his mercy and compassion.

CHAPTER 19 - A GIFT OF MERCY

MONDAY, MARCH 11

My family drove home on Sunday night to return to their jobs, but God, in his mercy, sent someone to help me get through the coming weeks. At the start of the Monday morning shift, a student nurse, dressed in a grey striped pinafore with a white blouse and matching stockings, breezed into the room. She appeared to be about my age. I estimated she was in her late twenties, or early thirties.

"Hi, I'm Amy, and I've been assigned to Kim for the day. I'll need to ask you a few questions."

She stood with a folder and pen in hand, and began asking one question after another. "What is her date of birth? Was Kim born premature or full term? List any childhood diseases. At what age did she learn to walk? Has she suffered a fall? When did she first present symptoms? What ...?"

My mind reeled from the incessant questioning which forced me to supply each minute detail of Kim's short life, and relive each horrible moment of our present nightmare. When the forms were at last complete, I breathed a sigh of relief.

Within the first hour of our introduction to one another, Amy entered our room for the second time pushing a portable bed to transport Kim to radiation therapy. I trembled with fear when we entered the elevator. The unknown still lurked within the walls of this hospital. Sensing my apprehension, Amy attempted to keep me engaged with trivial matters by enquiring about my hometown, my interests, and the weather. Regardless of the banal conversation, nothing could assuage the cold terror running through my veins the second those elevator doors opened, and I read the words on the door marked, "CAUTION, RADIATION AREA."

Amy placed Kim's medical file into the hands of the technician, who in turn summoned the radiologist. Dr. Kincaid escorted me into his office to explain the procedure. He meticulously outlined each step of the treatments and gave me detailed answers to each of my questions. Just before handing me a pen, he issued a final warning. "With treatments such as these, some tissue damage is inevitable."

I steadied my shaking hand long enough to sign the papers. I never imagined giving my consent to a treatment which could possibly cause further brain damage—or even more frightening—leave Kim in her present condition. Ultimately, I had no other choice. The alternative meant death, and we needed to do everything possible to save her.

On the second day of Kim's treatments, Amy invited me to lunch. Seldom thinking of food, I demurred. My mind was centered solely on taking care of Kim. My heart quivered at the thought of leaving her alone for any length of time.

Amy grasped my forearm and pulled me toward the door. "Come on," she insisted. "You need to eat."

While we sat at the table nibbling on salads from the buffet, Amy carried the conversation. "I just recently got divorced. With three children to support, I decided to become a nurse. By the way, I also have a little girl named Kim."

I smiled at the sweet coincidence. "Thank you for taking such good care of *my* Kim, and thank you for inviting me to lunch."

"Well, all the nurses have noticed you rarely eat unless your family is here. Besides, we have a lot in common, and we both want Kim to get well."

She scanned the area around our table then leaned toward me conspiratorially. "That's what I wanted to talk to you about. I'm going to ask my supervisor to assign me to Kim for the rest of my pediatric study. Student nurses are usually required to rotate to different patients, so she will have to grant me special permission."

"Amy, I can't think of a better arrangement. I hate going through the endless protocol and answering the same questions every day with each new nurse. But, more than anything, I appreciate how loving you are toward Kim."

"Keep your fingers crossed, I'm asking for permission at the end of my shift."

Although other student nurses were also allowed to observe Kim and write reports, thus continuing the daily question and answer sessions with me, the supervisor granted Amy's request and allowed her to complete her pediatric study attending Kim.

Two weeks later, Amy had just begun prepping Kim for her final day of prescribed radiation treatments when Dr. Carlton entered the room. He leaned over the guard rail and studied Kim at length before shifting his gaze toward me. "I've observed no significant changes in her condition. I'm sorry, but I believe it's useless to continue the radiation. I've cancelled today's treatment. I can't offer you any hope. The best thing now would be to place her in a nursing facility; leave her there, and go home to your other children."

I stood frozen in place. Although I worried about a myriad

of things concerning Kim, the thought of a nursing home never entered my mind. Kim was critically ill; she needed to be in a hospital. For anyone to believe we would consider placing her in a nursing home, both appalled and shocked me. His words sent shards of sickening despair to the pit of my stomach. She is only two years old!

Dr. Carlton's second implication also intensified my guilt over leaving my other children. Did the man not understand how much I grieved for my five-year-old son and newborn baby? No mother should be forced to choose between her children. Knowing Dirk and Kristi were being well cared for and nurtured by my parents was the only way I found it possible to cope with our situation. Dan saw them daily, but I was not oblivious to their need for me as well. I held on by compartmentalizing: Today my place is with Kim. Weekends are reserved for my other children.

Nothing about the situation was fair, but it was the best I could do. Amy, as visibly shaken as I, put her arms around me, and we cried together in shared grief. Blinking back tears, she insisted, "Let's go for a walk."

We stepped hand in hand down the two flights of stairs to the lobby then walked outside the hospital doors for fresh air. Neither of us spoke as we exited the building; too many thoughts rattled around in my brain for me to utter one word. Our walk came to an abrupt halt in the middle of the walkway when Amy asserted, "Marie, you know you don't want Kim to live like this forever."

"No, of course I don't! I have even asked God to take her if she can't be healed, but I just can't accept that it's God's will for her to die!"

Amy took my hand, and we trudged silently back up the steps to the third floor of the hospital. I rested my hope in God.

If Christ could raise Lazarus from the dead, then I believed he could certainly heal one small child. I entered our room and bent down to kiss Kim's forehead. "Kimmie, Mommy's here. I love you sweet baby girl."

I had no time to think about my worst fear. I needed to deal with another urgent matter. Dr. Carlton intended to transfer Kim on Monday, and he wanted the name of our chosen nursing facility as soon as possible. The idea of a nursing home both shocked and embittered me. I couldn't understand how the doctor could be so callous. Did he really expect us to place our child in an institution, forget about her, and return to our regular lives? I vowed to take care of Kim regardless of what anyone tried to do. No one was going to place her in a facility!

In retrospect, Dr. Carlton's reasoning was not predicated on cruelty and callousness; it only seemed so at the time. The doctor understood the impracticality of my being the sole caregiver. Kim required constant care—twenty-four hours of the day. He was concerned for my other children who needed a mother as well. Yet, I could not think beyond the threat of Kim's death, and the fact I needed to be with her as much as possible. I had years to be with my other children, but perhaps only weeks to spend with her.

Dr. Carlton admitted he could no longer predict how long Kim might live. "The tumor has either slowed or halted its growth. No distinguishable signs of further deterioration of the brain can be detected. Her condition has not altered over the preceding two weeks, conceivably because of the radiation."

I left Kim in Amy's excellent care while I sought a place of solitude. Sadness crippled me. From a quaking voice, I sent an anguished prayer to heaven. "Lord, with each new trial, I've declared, 'I cannot bear any more grief!' Yet, you've walked with me through each crisis and given me added strength. But today

Lord ... I beg of you ... please intervene. I can't place our little girl in a nursing home!

"It's almost as if they want me to put her away somewhere and forget she ever existed. Kim is my child! How can I walk away from her? What if she can hear me? What will happen when she no longer hears my voice beside her?

"Dear Lord, you gave Kimmie to me. It's bad enough to never be able to cuddle my infant or comfort my son, but now, I'm expected to place Kim in a facility, turn my back upon her, and walk away. Lord, I'm being pulled in every direction. Please Father, open a way for us. Do not allow circumstances to force me to make such a decision; I can't!"

Within the hour, the radiologist appeared in the doorway to say goodbye. "Mrs. Grissom, I am so sorry the treatments failed. I hoped Kim would be showing signs of improvement by now. I wish I could do more."

Tears dripped from his eyes while I pleaded with him for answers to my own anguish. "Why were the treatments stopped? Is Dr. Carlton afraid of what Kim will be like if she wakes up? How can I just give up and take her home to die?"

Dr. Kincaid had no answers for my questions; instead, he sadly shook his head while responding, "I am very sorry. I can only offer you my regrets."

The doctor could not bear to look at Kim, and I was puzzled by his reaction. How could a physician, who saw Kim only on rare occasions, be so touched? I discovered the answer to my quandary from Greg, another member of the radiology staff.

"I'm sorry Mrs. Grissom," he replied. "I assumed you already knew. Kim stole everyone's heart in the lab when she first arrived. We tried to comfort her, but she was frightened and in severe pain. Dr. Kincaid couldn't stand to see her cry, so he armed himself in protective gear, lifted Kim from the table, and held her in his lap throughout the entire process of X-rays and air studies before each surgery."

I steadied myself against the wall. My mind flashed back to the morning when Dan and I were forced to leave radiology while Kimmie screamed, *"Mommy, Daddy, don't leave me!"*

To know that when we exited the room, Dr. Kincaid swept Kimmie up in his arms and cradled her for hours on end, brought unprecedented peace to my heart. My baby didn't have to lie in terror on a menacingly cold table!

Dan drove up on Friday night. We spent the weekend mulling over our options, but any real plan eluded us. We could not willingly contemplate Dr. Carlton's directive, so we sought God for the answer.

From a medical perspective, we understood Dr. Carlton had no other choice. Kim no longer received any medical treatments other than physical care and feedings. The hospital would not allow Kim to occupy a room indefinitely. Yet, we could not imagine a scenario in which we assigned the care and well-being of our child to an institution. In fact, Dan's answer was straight-forward and simple. "We're not doing it! I don't care what anyone says!"

On Saturday morning, Amy breezed into the room. Her visit surprised us. She completed her last day of pediatric training on Friday.

"What are you doing here?" I inquired. "I thought you had the weekend off before you begin training on a new floor."

"There's something I need to tell you," she replied. "I want to take care of Kim as long as possible. If you decide to place Kim in your hometown hospital, then as soon as I complete my training, I'll go there and apply for a job. If you want to take Kim home, I'll come and be her nurse. All I ask in return is room and board."

Overwhelmed by her offer, we stumbled over an appropriate response. Dan spoke first. "Thank you. That's a mighty generous thing for you to do. We really appreciate it."

I tearfully hugged Amy and whispered, "I can't believe you're willing to do this with three children of your own to take care of and support. You are an answer to prayers, and I love you."

Amy stepped backward; her chestnut eyes bore into mine. "I need to tell you one more thing. This was my second time to train in Pediatrics. The Director of Nurses made me repeat it because one of the supervisors didn't like my work. I've always tried to do everything to the best of my ability, so I was devastated. But now I think I know the reason it happened.

"God wanted me here to take care of Kimmie. I know it's true because I have been drawn to Kim; I love her. It hurts to think of letting anyone else take care of her. She's healed a part of me that's been bitter ever since my divorce. I see life through different eyes because of her."

We agreed with Amy. God placed her in the perfect position. How else could I have been able to get through the long weeks and trying days without Amy? My family could not be with me on a daily basis. Collect, long distant phone calls were stretching an already thin budget. If Kim had not needed Amy, I certainly did.

After Amy's departure, Dan and I discussed our options. Our decision involved so much more than where we placed Kim. We not only had financial considerations; but we also needed to determine the best plan for all three of our children. Kristi deserved her mother's full attention, and we worried about how

Dirk might be affected by seeing Kim in her present condition day after day. More importantly, we needed to determine how we could circumvent his presence when Kim's moment with death arrived.

At least we now had another option. If we took Kim home, Amy was willing to assist us with her round-the-clock care. Nevertheless, we questioned whether we should ask a mother of three to make such a sacrifice.

After kissing his little girl goodbye, Dan drove home late Sunday night. In the end, we decided to transfer Kim back to our local hospital until we could make other arrangements. When we were home and together as a family, it might be possible to see things from a clearer perspective. Secretly however, I prayed, "Lord, please intervene in our situation. Give us wisdom, and show us the way."

CHAPTER 20 - MIRACLE ON
THE THIRD FLOOR

The emotional tug of war over the weekend left me physically exhausted. I sought oblivion to quell the voices in my head. At two o'clock in the morning, I lay fitfully napping on the pull-out bed when a nurse stepped into the room to take Kim's vital signs. Unable to shake off my fatigue long enough to acknowledge her presence, I closed my eyes to drift once more on the waves of my fears.

Within moments, the sound of other nurses entering the room and voices rising above the accustomed whispers, penetrated my weary fog. I shot up from the bed with dread filling my soul. Nurses gaped back at me with smiles spread across their faces. I stared in disbelief when the nurses shouted in unison, "Kim's eyes are reacting to light!"

The entire nursing staff filled the room. Each stood around the bed waiting for a turn to flash the light in Kim's eyes and watch her pupils constrict. Although the nurses made a valiant effort, they simply could not hide their joy under the guise of professionalism.

God's goodness overwhelmed me. Just as the doctor offered

no hope, our heavenly Father poured out a blessing upon his tiny creation. I could neither contain my joy nor fully comprehend God's amazing love. I sat on a tall stool beside Kim, tightly holding her hand in mine, while silently rejoicing and thanking God for his mercy.

Only hours before, I spent the evening preparing Kim to leave me in death. If only a miniscule chance existed that she could hear my voice, I wanted to help her understand the circumstances. "Kimmie, God is just resting your eyes and body so you can get well. One day soon you will wake up and never be sick again."

My words conveyed the truth. Should death befall her, sickness could never invade her body again. Yet, in this moment of God's perfect timing, with the sun still only a promise in the eastern sky, I found myself whispering words of God's sustaining love to my daughter. "Kim, it's all right; you are just waking up. Someday soon you will be well again. Jesus is taking care of you sweetheart."

With renewed hope, I believed Kim's healing was imminent, and her home was with us, instead of in heaven.

I waited as long as I could to phone Dan. I didn't want to call early and alarm him, but as the hands of time approached six o'clock in the morning, I couldn't contain my excitement a moment longer. When he answered the phone, I greeted him with the words, "Our miracle is happening. Kim is waking up!"

I sat beside Kim expectantly waiting hour after hour for her to open her eyes, but nothing dramatic happened throughout the day. At times her eyes reacted to light; other times they did not. She must be waking up, I reasoned. Why isn't she opening her eyes?

When the long day ended, and midnight fell, I was forced to give up my minute by minute vigil. My shoulders ached, and my head throbbed from sitting beside Kim for over twenty hours. I unfolded the bed, and stacked pillows on one end to elevate my head enough to view her from across the room, but the dim light only allowed me to see a shadow of her face. I reclined, stretching my aching body, but I could not sleep; instead, I watched the clock. With the passing of each fifteen minute interval, I rose to check on Kim. I didn't want her to wake up thinking she was alone.

Tuesday's morning sun penetrated the room. Kim's eyes remained closed. The nurses appeared subdued. They had expected greater progress as well.

I prayed, "Lord, you created the stars by your word, and brought man to life with your breath. Surely you can do all things!"

When it was time for the linens to be changed, I placed my hands under Kim to lift her from the bed. In recent weeks, lifting her had been no small task. Because her body lay limp and her limbs and head hung heavily, each part of her body needed to be supported with my hands and arms. But this time, I lifted her with ease. Her body was less flaccid than in previous days. I carried her across the room. Kim's arms remained folded across her chest; they did not dangle lifelessly at her side. I sat down in the rocking chair to cradle her close to my heart.

"Kimmie, I'm here honey. I know you are waking up. I can't wait to see your big blue eyes."

When I clasped Kim's right hand in mine, her index finger trembled against my palm. *"O Lord, thank you!"*

I brought her hand to my lips and bestowed a kiss. Her finger trembled once more.

"I can feel your finger moving Kimmie Dawn. I know you hear me! I love you sweetie."

Unfortunately, I was the only one who held Kim, and the

only one who received a response; no one else noticed the inconspicuous changes. Very few wanted to believe an overly anxious mother, and Dr. Carlton topped the list of unbelievers. Neither did he put much faith in the nurses' reports about Kim's response to light. Many of the nurses had become emotionally involved with her, and because the doctor never saw a visible change in Kim's condition, he could not be convinced without credible evidence. He was determined to send her home without further treatment.

I waited each morning for Dr. Carlton to arrive and announce plans for Kim's transfer, but those dreaded words were never mentioned until his visit on Wednesday morning.

"Our office hasn't been able to reach Dr. Paul. Each time we call, he is unavailable. We will keep calling, but if I don't get a response soon, the transfer will not be possible before next week."

When Dr. Carlton exited the room, I smiled with relief. Dr. Paul's "unavailability" gave Kim more time to wake up! As far as I was concerned, his inability to connect with our local physician demonstrated God's perfect timing. Kimmie's immediate caregivers were beginning to observe discernable changes in her appearance.

Dr. Carlton made his rounds on Thursday morning with no mention of the transfer. By midafternoon of the same day, two newly assigned nurses, Betty and Sarah, watched Kim respond to the sound of my voice with a tiny fluttering of her long lashes.

Betty instructed, "Ask her to squeeze your hand. Let's see if she can follow commands."

I obeyed by positioning Kim's hand across the center of my open palm. "Kimmie, do you feel my hand? Try to squeeze my hand honey." She didn't respond.

"Kimmie, if you can hear me, please try to squeeze my hand. I know you can do it."

Kim's index finger trembled just before her hand scrunched slightly in an attempt to squeeze my hand. I swiveled my head toward the nurses. Each wore a smile. The movement was miniscule, but they observed the scant quickening of Kim's hand.

"That's a really good sign," Sarah admitted. Betty nodded in agreement.

That moment became a turning point. Kim began working determinedly to open her eyes. She often remained awake in spans of thirty minutes or longer with her long lashes fluttering continuously. Nurses, visitors, and perfect strangers stood nearby to watch her heavy eyelids flitter. Everyone ... with the exception of Dr. Carlton ... saw her waking up. Each time the doctor came by on morning and evening rounds, Kim lay in a deep sleep.

By Friday morning, our time was running short. Dr. Carlton planned to make arrangements to send us home without further delay. I asked one of the nurses to sit with Kim while I went to the chapel. I stepped to my familiar spot behind the last pew, knelt down, and poured my heart out to God.

"Lord, you must be waking Kim for a reason. If the treatments are the cause of her improvement, sending her home could lead to her death. Father, I believe you can heal without radiation or drugs. I'm leaving it in your hands. If she wakes up at home, no one can doubt your great power, but Lord, if you want us to stay here, I will trust you to find a way. Whether you heal Kim, or take her home with you, I will eternally praise your name."

I scurried up the stairs to our room, and sat down to wait. Within ten minutes, the doctor appeared on his morning rounds. Dr. Carlton briefly glanced in Kim's direction before making his announcement. "I am preparing to call Dr. Paul within the hour."

Fear gripped my heart. My anxiety rendered me speechless until an inner force urged me to fight for my child. "Dr. Carlton, Kim is waking up! She is constantly trying to open her eyes, and she can squeeze my hand when I ask her."

He stared incredulously at me, then challenged, "Show me."

I slowly shuffled to the bed with my head whirling in defeat. Shortly before the doctor arrived, I tried to awaken Kim by calling her name while I stroked her hand and arm, but she didn't respond. I knew she had momentarily drifted back into a deep sleep. On rare occasions she could be roused by external stimulation, but for the most part, she awoke through her own volition. I lifted her limp arm. My heart sank. Kim resided in a faraway slumber where I could not reach her.

I patted her hand while calling her name. "Kimmie! Kimmie Dawn, can you hear me? It's Mom, honey. Wake up!"

She made no response.

Betty stood beside me. Understanding my desperation, she pulled her ballpoint pen from the pocket of her uniform, and ran it across the bottom of Kim's right foot.

Dr. Carlton watched as Kim's toes curled from the stimulation, then bluntly stated, "That is simply an involuntary reflex; it proves nothing."

As if in response to Dr. Carlton's statement, Kim's right leg instantly rose six inches from the bed. I watched in stunned disbelief. Over the course of the week, I witnessed a minuscule movement of her hand, but this was amazing!

While I held my breath, the doctor watched mutely, and betrayed nothing for what seemed like an eternity. With his eyes focused squarely on Kim, he at last spoke. "I will order two more weeks of radiation therapy."

Without further conversation, Dr. Carlton marched from the room as abruptly as he had appeared. Still unconvinced, he simply decided upon giving in to a mother's desperate attempt to save her child.

Mere seconds following his exit; Kim's eyes began to flutter rapidly. I jerked to attention, looked toward the nurses' station, and saw the doctor jotting down notes at the counter.

I flew to the door and shouted, "Dr. Carlton, Kim is opening her eyes!"

The doctor jolted upright, and much to my surprise, ran at full speed into the room. I swerved from his pathway just in time to avoid a collision. He watched as Kim bravely fought to keep her eyelids from closing.

I was much too busy speaking to Kim while trying to hold her attention to notice Dr. Carlton's expression. I only heard the enthusiastic words, "ALL RIGHT!"

Later, the nurses in attendance told me he exited the room beaming with joy. His reaction astonished me. In spite of his demeanor and blunt speech, Dr. Carlton didn't want to give up on Kim. His heart, like ours, was rooted in seeing our daughter respond to the treatments.

I could only praise God for his mercy. Surely he intended for us to stay at this hospital so Kim could be healed. I ran to the phone to tell Dan the wonderful news.

Before going back to Pediatrics, I stopped by the chapel to thank the one most responsible for my joy.

"Father, how can I possibly thank you for what you just did? It would have been impossible for me to rouse Kim without your help. She lifted her leg! I can't believe her leg rose at the exact moment Dr. Carlton doubted every word I said.

"Lord, everything I just witnessed was the work of your hands; there is no other explanation. You revealed your power and glory today; nothing could ever match the grace you have bestowed upon us. Kimmie is coming back! Thank you Father. Thank you."

CHAPTER 21 - GOD'S
ABUNDANT PROVISION

We often focus so much on our own needs and desires that we fail to see God's plan in the making. If we are not vigilant, we miss opportunities of divine appointment.

I exited the chapel and jogged up the stairs to Pediatrics. I had work to do. The hospital was in the process of renovating several of its floors, and the pediatric patients were being moved to another wing of the hospital.

My having to pack everything in the room in preparation for the move somewhat stifled my joy over Kim's recent deliverance. I looked at the dozens of beautiful gowns, the assemblage of encouraging cards and letters, two shelves of dolls and stuffed animals, along with a third shelf of books. My clothes filled the small closet. Each of these items must be taken to the car and stored until we could be assigned a new room.

Stacks of things needed to be moved, and it was a long trip down two flights of stairs, followed by a winding hallway which led out to the parking lot. The elevator was available, but I wanted time alone to savor every moment. Kim was scheduled to receive more life-saving treatments. Nothing else mattered.

Betty kept watch over Kim while I moved our things. When I returned from my first trip to the car, a young woman with auburn hair and green eyes stood to the right of the bed looking down at my child. Two nights earlier she and her husband had rushed their baby to the hospital with a high temperature. I wasn't entirely certain I wanted her in the room with Kim.

On Thursday, this same woman stood across the hall multiple times throughout the day watching Kim through the large observation window. She returned to peer at us again in the early hours of the night. Each time I saw her, she appeared visibly upset. Although by now I had become accustomed to the curiosity and pity generated by the sight of Kim in a coma, her presence concerned me.

The woman introduced herself as "Gina," and kindly offered to help me carry my things to the car. I refused in most part because I needed the time to be alone with Jesus to thank him for his wonderful mercy. With each return trip, I found Gina standing beside Kim's bed and speaking with the nurse.

I appreciated Betty's presence; for once I did not have to answer the latest round of extensive questioning. I found it difficult, and often impossible, to inform virtual strangers about Kim's illness and prognosis. Each inquirer asked the inevitable question: "How can you stand to be in this room watching her?"

I answered with my own question: "I love her. How could I *stand* to be away from her?"

With predictability, the same questions unalterably followed the first. "When did you first notice she was ill? Has she had it long? Can't they do anything?"

The move, along with the presence of a very loving nurse, gave me a reprieve from these endless questions.

By two o'clock in the afternoon, Kim and I were situated in our new surroundings on the second floor of the hospital's south wing. Because of the renovations, the entire pediatric ward moved to an unused portion of the hospital which once served as a dormitory for aspiring LVN students. Our room was much smaller than before, but the bright sunshine cascading from the south windows more than made up for the lack of space. At last we were offered a modicum of privacy because the former encroaching "window to the world" was a thing of the past.

The move obviously disturbed Kim; she spent more than two hours desperately working to open her beautiful eyes. Coincidentally, she exhibited such great progress just two days before her third birthday.

I completed the finishing touches on our room a few moments before Betty appeared on her hourly rounds to check Kim. After writing her report, she looked toward me. "Come with me. I have a surprise for you."

Of all the nurses assigned to Pediatrics, Betty possessed a heart of gold. She exuded love for her young patients beneath an exterior of pure professionalism. Dressed in a crisp, white uniform with a starched white cap perched primly upon her head, she led me down the hall past an adjoining corridor, and stopped at the third door to her left. A bright smile lit up her face while she motioned for my silence, and quietly pushed the door open. I followed her inside and stood in shock. I looked upon a massive room with long rows of sinks, toilets, and shower stalls in working condition.

With a wink, Betty confided, "We are keeping this a secret. At one time, this was the student restroom and shower area. Since we've moved from the pediatric floor, it will serve as the nurses' restroom, and will be off limits to the public. However, all of the nurses gathered for a meeting, and we unanimously decided to share it with you."

Betty folded her arms across her waist and smiled. "You are welcome to use this facility any time. In fact, we thought it might be the perfect place for you to bathe. You won't have to drive across town every day to your relatives' home for a quick shower, and then rush back to the hospital."

Surely God had just reached down and brushed me with a kiss. The bathroom looked the same as the one in my first college dorm. Stark, and offering little privacy, its green- tiled walls and floors echoed with each step we took. Obviously built to meet basic human needs without regard to aesthetics, it could at best, be described as utilitarian. Nevertheless, in my present circumstances, I stood in the most beautiful room I had ever seen.

Gary and Beth graciously offered their home to me for daily showers and rest. I appreciated their hospitality, but trying to schedule my absence from the hospital around radiation treatments, doctor visits, feedings, and Kim's general care had become increasingly difficult. With Kim's new, budding alertness, I found it even more challenging to leave. I never wanted my child to think I abandoned her. Now, thanks to the generosity of these wonderful nurses, I no longer had to worry about leaving Kim. Everything I needed was within a short walk.

When Betty and I stepped out into the hall, the Director of Nurses joined us with one more surprise. "Mrs. Grissom, this wing is completely separated from the rest of the hospital and has a direct outside entrance. We think it would be appropriate to allow your entire family, including your children, access to our waiting room for visits."

Betty quickly added, "We realize each time your parents come, someone must wait outside the hospital with your other children. We're tired of seeing your family separated, so now you can bring everyone up here where you'll all be comfortable."

God's beautiful angels of mercy surrounded me. I could

only thank these two via my tears. Unworthiness welled up in my soul. I had done nothing to deserve the compassion these caring nurses bestowed upon me.

Others constantly inquired, "Where is God in all of this?" The answer seemed so simple to me. His presence manifested itself in every comforting word from a friend, in each prayer, and in every act of kindness from strangers. Now, I saw God's handprint indelibly stamped upon the actions of these nurses who had just given me two precious gifts.

I left Kim in Betty's capable hands while I took a short walk outside. I needed time to reflect upon the day. The blinding spring sun beamed down upon the earth as the Holy Spirit reminded me of God's unfathomable love. Kim's illness placed a heavy burden upon each member of my family, but this journey was not just about the pain in our hearts, but rather about God's abundant provision for us in the midst of our suffering. I marveled at the way in which he met our needs at the exact time we were desperate for his help.

When I strolled past the front entrance of the hospital, I peered upward. Catching a glimpse of the window of Kim's former room in Pediatrics, I recalled the day when I sat reading my Bible while Kim slept. My heart cried out, "Lord, I am so lonely and afraid!"

Within moments of my prayer, a shadow cast itself over the doorway. Startled, I looked up, and recognized the tall frame of my brother bending over Kim's bed. Wes lived hundreds of miles from our home, and he and his wife were expecting their second child in a matter of weeks. I didn't expect him to leave his family at this critical time in their lives to make such a long trip.

I quickly jumped to my feet while Wes took two long strides across the room to gather me into his arms. He didn't need to say a word; the strength I needed so desperately flowed from him into my spirit giving me the will to continue. Our circumstances had not changed, but my brother was the exact person I needed. He not only gave me courage, but he also gave renewed strength to my parents. As I thought about that day, as well as all the other times in which God supplied our needs, I whispered quick words of praise before returning to Kim.

Shortly after eight o'clock in the evening, the opportunity I refused earlier, presented itself again. I sat beside Kim reading aloud her favorite book when I heard a light tapping at the door. Looking up, I watched Gina enter the room. Obviously, something troubled her. She fidgeted inside the doorway.

After exhaling at length, she found the courage to speak. "I've come to apologize."

Gina eyed the floor. "I felt so foolish standing outside your daughter's room just staring at the two of you, but I couldn't help myself! For some reason I was drawn to the window, and I couldn't leave. I have another son just a little older than Kim, and I kept imagining what it would be like if my little Tad was lying there."

Setting her gaze squarely on me, she extended her hands with palms upward in a pleading position. "I've watched you sit beside her hour after hour—talking and singing as if nothing is wrong. If that was my child I would be hysterical! I need to ask you just one question. How do you do it?"

Her question shook me. The words she spoke were not new, but something was different about her inquiry. I sensed real concern. Rising from my chair, I motioned her to follow me into the hallway. When we were safely away from Kim's hearing, I calmly proffered my routine answer. "God unfailingly supplies the strength I need."

Gina implored, "It makes no sense to me! She is so beautiful. How can you sit there knowing she might die, and keep yourself from falling to pieces?"

My thoughts raced back in time to the beginning days of Kim's illness when I shrank into a weeping and wailing ball of self-pity. I smiled in amazement. How could anyone believe I was a tower of strength?

In answer to Gina's plea, I shared my secret. "My formula for courage is simply to walk to a secluded place and cry until there is nothing left inside, then ask God to do everything according to his will. Lastly, before entering Kim's room again, I pray for the strength to overcome my fears so my daughter will never know how frightened and upset I am."

"But I still don't see how you do it," she cried. "I know I couldn't!"

"No one can do it. No mother in the world can watch her child suffer without crumbling under the heartache. Jesus Christ is the only answer. If you have Jesus in your life, you can trust him to get you through any situation. No matter what the outcome may be, he assures you everything will be all right. It's rough; it's agonizing, but God is my comfort and my strength. I can't depend upon anything else or even another person to get me through this. Jesus is the only one who can."

Gina's baby was dismissed from the hospital the following morning, but before leaving, she dropped in to say goodbye. Once again, I thought very little about her visit, for I had become accustomed to the steady flow of parents and children entering and leaving the hospital. In the coming weeks I seldom thought of Gina; too many other surrounding activities consumed me.

CHAPTER 22 - BIRTHDAY BLESSINGS

SATURDAY, MARCH 30

Gina's farewell delayed my own plans. I hurried to pack for an overnight visit with my family. Today was Dirk's sixth birthday. The following day would mark Kim's third year on earth, but I tried not to think about it.

The nurses asked about purchasing a cake for Kim, but I begged them to wait until she could celebrate the event with us. I could not bear the thought of everyone standing around eating cake while my child could neither eat nor drink.

"Once Kim is better," I promised, "we will celebrate her birthday in earnest."

With the progress she was making, I believed it might be possible for our special celebration to occur within a matter of weeks. I envisioned Kim eating her fill of chocolate cake while hugging a new doll. A green riding toy, in the shape of a huge worm, would be close by, waiting for the day when Kim was strong enough to sit upon it. Please God; let it happen!

I left Kim in the safe-keeping of Dan's parents. They graciously offered to sit with Kim on weekends while I rested and spent time with my other children. One of Dan's sisters drove up on Wednesdays to give me respite as well. But, I never stopped yearning to be with Kim, and I never ceased worrying. She's waking up! What if she asks for me?

I didn't know how much longer I could continue to make these weekend trips back home. I welcomed every family member to come and spend time with Kim, but I should be with her as much as possible now. Whether she woke up, returned to her old self, or took a downward turn, I needed to be with her. I had missed too many of her battles. I didn't want Kim to ever be forced again to ask, *"Where is Mom?"*

Yet, in spite of my resolve, two other children needed my attention as well. I didn't have an answer for my dilemma.

I packed Dirk's gifts safely in the trunk, then drove to the bakery. Earlier in the week, I ordered a western-themed cake decorated with cowboys, horses, and a corral. I carefully secured the cake in the trunk along with the gifts and drove home. This same road grew longer with each trip. Whether I traveled home, or back to the hospital, I left a child behind.

Dan and I plastered smiles on our faces, and playfully teased and pampered our son while we celebrated his birthday. We sang to him, while with one puff, our six-year-old blew out the candles on his cake. He opened gifts of clothing, games, and new toys, but I saved the best gift for last.

Dirk ripped the wrapping paper from a long, narrow box, and opened one end to peek inside. "Cool!" he exclaimed while pulling the gift from its box. "This gun is just like Daniel Boone's! Thanks."

"We wanted to get you something special honey," I answered. "There should be caps in the box that go with it. Dad and I hope you know how much we love you. I'm sorry we couldn't give you a real party."

"Son, we just couldn't do it this year with Kim being in the hospital," Dan added.

"I know," Dirk replied. "But Mom, I'm glad you're home."

My heart melted. I gathered him in my arms for a hug. "I'm so very glad I'm home too, honey. I love you. Happy Birthday."

Dirk ran off to try out each of his toys. "Come on Dad," he shouted. "Let's play. We're burning daylight!"

I took the baby from Dan's arms so he could spend time with his son. Cradling my newborn, I inspected every inch of God's precious gift in an attempt to memorize each tiny feature.

"Hello little one. It's your birthday too; I can't believe you are five weeks old today. Mommy's missed you!"

I rubbed my thumb across her chin; Kristi endearingly smiled.

"Oh, it's the first time I've seen your sweet smile. I've missed so many other firsts in your short life. I'm sorry baby. I love you Kristi Lynne!"

We took the traditional birthday snapshots, but one child's face was missing from the photos, and we each sensed our loss. Last year on his birthday, Dirk insisted he and Kimmie celebrate together by opening presents and simultaneously blowing out the candles on their cake. Both children loved the start of what we thought would become a tradition each year in our home.

Unspoken questions floated in the room. Will this scene be repeated forever? Will only one child be present throughout the years to blow out the candles and rip the paper from the pile of gifts? Will the following day … Kim's official birthday … be forever empty and void of any celebration? How many children will we see in the birthday pictures?

After singing lullabies and rocking Kristi to sleep, I cuddled Dirk and spent the remainder of the night giving him the attention he deserved. We played games, read books, and talked for hours. At bedtime, I tucked my son into bed and kissed him goodnight.

The four of us, along with my parents, returned early Sunday morning to celebrate Kim's third birthday. My heart ached with an indescribable sadness. Today should be the first birthday she could really celebrate while understanding its significance. We should be celebrating with joy while we watched Kim blow out the candles arm in arm with her brother. Instead, she lay helpless in a hospital bed.

With Dr. Carlton so determined to send her home without further treatments, I gave Kim a special gift one week earlier. I couldn't be certain she would live to receive it on her birthday, so I purchased a birthstone ring with a brilliant aquamarine stone centered in a band of sterling silver, and slipped it on her finger. Its pale blue color could not match the intensity of her brilliant sapphire eyes, but it was an answer to her heart's desire.

On a shopping trip in early January, she spied a similar ring in the display window of our local jeweler and exclaimed, "Look at the blue ring, Mom! It is so pretty. Can I have it? I want a ring to wear just like you."

After giving Kim the ring, I resolved to forgo any other gifts until she could enjoy every moment of the festivities. Others had not felt the same way. As soon as we arrived at the hospital, I walked down the hall to check on Kim while the rest of my family settled themselves in the lobby. At first glance, I thought I had entered the wrong room.

Balloon bouquets floated throughout the space. Cards lined the shelf beneath the window, and the bedside table housed a glittering gift box with a beautiful pink gown embellished with lace and ribbon. The matching sheer robe was spread across the end of Kim's bed. An attached card read, "With all our love, Grandma and Grandpa."

I could almost see her at home modeling the beautiful gown. Her first twirl would be made directly in front of Dan while she inquired, "Daddy, aren't I pretty?"

Nurses dressed Kim in a tulip pink gown and matching knit cap; the birthstone ring glistened on her finger. One pink balloon bobbed at the foot of her bed. The staff pooled their resources to purchase the balloons and a cuddly stuffed poodle with a bright pink bow tied around its neck. Betty placed the mini puppy lovingly astride the bed rail at just the right angle for Kim to see when opening her eyes. I loved each of these women for caring so much. God bless nurses who get involved!

I returned to the lobby, and held Kristi while Dirk snuggled close by. Dan and my parents walked down the hall to have their first uninterrupted visit with Kim in weeks. Minutes ticked by. "Father," I silently whispered, "thank you for these blessings! For the first time since Kimmie's hospital admittance, we are visiting as a family."

My parents were at last able to spend more time with their granddaughter than had ever been possible before. Who could have imagined that moving into an old, neglected dormitory could be so wonderful?

After thirty minutes, Mother and Dad emerged from the room. Dad wiped away tears, while Mother batted her eyes to prevent them from tearing up. The difference in Kim's appearance astounded them. Her countenance had changed; she projected an alertness.

Dad sat down beside me. "Baby, you told us Kim was getting better, but I had to see her with my own eyes before I could believe it. We have a gracious heavenly Father."

I placed Kristi in my mother's waiting arms, and took Dirk's hand to lead him to his sister. The hospital granted him one brief visit with her shortly after she fell into the coma, but three weeks had passed since that visit. Dan stood beside the bed, gazing upon his sweet little girl, and holding her hand. He beckoned his son to join him.

Dirk thrilled my heart when he trotted to her bed, took one look, then turned toward me in amazement, and declared, "Hey, she looks like the old Kim!"

At the sound of Dirk's voice, Kim desperately fought to open her eyes. I detected a miniscule movement of her hand before Dirk gently intertwined his fingers with hers. "Hey, Kim, you're getting better. Happy Birthday!"

In spite of my earlier protests, I couldn't let the day pass without recognizing her birthday; it might very well be her last. The three of us gathered around the bed. Dirk ripped the pink foil from the box and pulled out a new doll, also dressed in pink, to present to his sister. Of necessity, this doll could not be the same as the one she carried around so lovingly at home. Her new baby was made of cloth, rather than vinyl, to make it more lightweight and less irritating to Kim's delicate skin.

I placed the doll over her heart in the same position she always carried her baby—close enough to give continuous hugs and kisses. "Kimmie, this is your birthday baby. She has blond hair and big blue eyes just like you. It's from Dirk, Daddy, and me. We love you very much honey."

I moved Kim's right arm across her body and placed her hand upon the doll. Dirk reached for that same hand and held it gently in his. I stood in the middle of our family circle with my arms around the two men in my life, while Dan held Kim's left hand. Dirk sang a song to celebrate her birthday. I could almost see Kim dancing to his music.

I treasured this special moment, made even more significant by Dirk's presence. From this time forward, Kim invariably became more alert when her brother was near. I imagine she had dozens of things she wanted to say to Dirk, but his being in the room and standing beside her was Kim's greatest birthday gift of all.

CHAPTER 23 - THE SICK AND BROKEN

Kim began her new series of radiation treatments on Monday, the first day of April, and I immersed myself in the business of keeping her well and alert. Her skin had become tender from the long days of immobility, and the possibility of her developing pressure sores became a real threat. As a result, the beautiful robe and gown she received as a birthday gift from Mary and J.D., hung decoratively on the rail at the foot of her bed.

Betty advised me, "It's best to limit Kim's attire to soft knit shirts which hug the body, and keep wrinkles to a minimum. The slightest wrinkle could cause a mark or bruise, and we want to avoid any trauma to the skin as much as possible."

Thus I kept myself busy remaking the necks of her t-shirts so they could slip easily over her head, and hand stitching matching knit caps. But more importantly, I spent hour upon hour holding Kim while pressing her sweet body close to my heart.

The unit clerk, Liz, along with nurses, Sarah and Betty, became my support team. I depended upon having either Sarah or Betty assigned to Kim each day, and I looked forward to their companionship as well as the gentle care they provided. These three stopped by each morning on their break and again at lunch insisting I go with them to the coffee shop. "You need to eat so you can keep up your strength," they reminded.

Timmy, a leukemia patient, with sandy-blond hair and haunting brown eyes, appeared in our room each afternoon. Eying the books perched on the shelf beneath the window, the six-year-old inquired, "Can we read?"

Without waiting for an answer, he climbed onto the rocking chair and sat beside me while I held Kim. I pushed back the yearning to have Dirk sitting in that spot instead of Timmy. This little boy had no one. *Did Dirk feel just as abandoned as Timmy?*

Doctors admitted the boy into the hospital shortly before Kim's arrival. He seldom received a visit from any of his family. The mother invariably found an excuse to avoid visiting her ailing child. Word spread that she couldn't cope with his illness, so she turned to alcohol to dull the pain.

Timmy often dialed his home phone to speak with his mother. During those calls, I could hear his wailing pleas as they wafted down the hall. "Mommy please! Come see me! I miss you!"

The shy little boy timidly stepped into Kim's room after each phone call, and snuggled up beside me. When the sadness overcame him, I took Timmy down to the coffee shop for an ice cream treat. I couldn't replace his mother; I could only offer a distraction.

In the following weeks I witnessed the arrival of many critically ill and suffering children. I spoke to the parents of a six-month-old baby with a liver ailment who was not expected to survive until his first birthday. I watched a teenage girl being wheeled down the hall after surgery to remove a brain tumor.

I visited with the mother of another teenage girl who was born deaf. "Emily refuses to let her disability stand in her way.

I am so proud of her, but she has pushed herself beyond the breaking point to remain at the top of her class," she tearfully admitted.

I prayed with the family of a five-year-old boy who entered the hospital for the second time with brain cancer. Six months prior, a neurosurgeon cut away part of the vicious malignancy, but this time surgery was not an option. After numerous tests, his doctor sent the boy home advising, "Nothing more can be done."

Seeing these tragedies made me cuddle Kimmie closer each day while I treasured every minute I spent with her.

Sadly, I witnessed the admission of neglected, undernourished, and unkempt children. An utmost sorrow filled my heart when I held a three-month-old baby who weighed a mere five pounds. Nurses termed her malady, "*failure to thrive,*" when they placed the baby in my arms. "We're hoping this baby will feel a love from you her own mother can't provide."

How I wanted to shake these mothers! Couldn't they understand how fortunate they were to have children to care for and love?

Yet, to the glory of God, even though the things I witnessed sickened my heart, they ripped the blinders from me, and unveiled God's greater precepts. The world did not revolve around me and my pain. Our family was not singled out. Thousands of children throughout the world become ill each day; many die. No one should interpret this to mean God doesn't care, or that He loves these little ones and their families less!

While I watched mothers become emotional cripples or alcoholics rather than face the eventual death of their children, I recognized that without Jesus, I too, would become a victim of my own destructive pathway. After weeks of heartache and struggle, I ultimately realized I now had a better answer to the question visitors asked on a daily basis: "How do you stand it?"

When I walked down the church aisle at the age of ten to receive Christ as my Savior, Jesus walked beside me. Not only did I promise to love and honor Jesus, but He also made a commitment to live in me, to be my strength and my defender against all enemies. He promised to be my shield in all circumstances. I did not need to ask Christ for strength; He *was* my strength. Without Christ, my life would be in perpetual turmoil.

CHAPTER 24 - JESUS SEEKS
THE BROKENHEARTED

God is able to move men, change circumstances, or transform any heart in order to bring his plans to fruition ... even when we fight his leading.

My heavenly Father intended to use Kim as a catalyst to bring comfort and healing to others despite my reluctance. I often refused to be a willing participant in God's plan because changes were required before others could become a part of our lives. I wanted the very best for my child, and I adamantly considered Sarah and Betty *the very best* when it came to giving care to my daughter. I trusted their years of experience. These two nurses were professional, gentle, and kind; most importantly, they loved Kim.

Following Amy's departure, I spoke to the Director of Nurses. "Please don't assign another student nurse to Kim. Each student has been very respectful and kind. I have no complaints; I simply don't want to start over with someone new each day."

"Kim's illness is complex and rare," she answered. "Her case offers a great educational opportunity for students."

"But their opportunity comes in the form of a complete case study, which requires a thorough medical history, followed by a long list of questions. I just don't want to answer any more questions." Had I not answered these same, heart-rending queries enough?

She clasped her hands together forming a steeple, then paused in thought before replying, "I can't make any promises, but I will seriously consider your request."

I thanked her for her kindness, but walked away with a cloud of uncertainty hanging over my head. I cringed each time a new student struggled to master the techniques of lifting and turning a paralyzed child. I wanted those days behind me.

Regardless of my plea, the director assigned a new student to Kim's case—not just for one day—but for an unspecified period of time. The new arrangement didn't please me in the least, and to make matters worse, the student seemed very nervous and preoccupied. Her hands trembled with fear each time she touched Kim.

I expressed my concerns to Sarah and Betty, but they asked me to give her another chance. "We think she will be much better tomorrow. The first day is always the most stressful. New students have so much to learn in a very short period of time," Betty answered.

On the following day, the student appeared even more jittery and inept, but by the third day, I began to see a slight improvement in her performance. I grudgingly decided to stop fighting her presence. Perhaps with practice, she could become a good nurse.

I didn't know it at the time, but this student was another part of God's plan. Jesus sought her out and brought her to the very place she did not want to be.

May, a tall, middle-aged woman with greying hair, entered the nursing program to fill a void in her life. She and her husband had never been able to have children of their own. So now, with time on her hands, she wanted to do something to help others.

Before long our conversation naturally turned toward Kim and her illness. May admitted, "I didn't want to be assigned to Kim. In fact, I spent the better part of the first day talking with my supervisor about making a change. I even asked to be relieved of all pediatric duty."

I understood why she might not want to be assigned to Kim, but her last request puzzled me until she shared her personal story.

"When my husband and I married, he was a widower with a seven-year-old daughter named Kathy, and a three-year-old son named Jeff. I spent the following six years caring for those children as if they were my own. One day the doorbell rang. Jeff's baseball coach stood at the door. He told me there had been a terrible accident. Jeff was riding home on his bicycle after baseball practice when a car struck and killed him.

"Since the day we lost our little boy, it just seems like every child I've ever known has been shrouded in some kind of tragedy. My sister has lost two children, and now my eighteen-year-old stepdaughter is slowly losing her sight from an eye disease. Since Jeff's death, I've never been able to relate to other children. I won't allow myself to love another child because it will only lead to pain and sorrow."

What a tragedy! The life of one small boy was suddenly snuffed out, and in that frozen segment of time, May's life became a shamble as well. With the great number of children currently on the pediatric floor, she couldn't believe the director assigned her to a child who could also be headed toward the same outcome. But, with each passing day, I saw subtle changes in May. I witnessed her anxiety lessen, and before long she became just as involved in Kim's progress as the other nurses.

To my surprise, she chose Kim for her formal case study. Because of the complexity of Kim's illness, it became a long and detailed study. Other cases required less work, but she chose Kim in order to spend more time with her. And yes, I answered those same heart-rending questions, along with additional ones. This was God's pathway—not mine.

My heart rejoiced one morning when May confessed, "I no longer think of Kim as a condemned child. Caring for her has helped me overcome my fear of becoming involved with children. When I look at Kim, I only see a child who radiates God's love."

God's grace, flowing through Kim, healed May's broken heart and gave her a new understanding of God's love in *all* things.

Chapter 25 - A Promise Realized

No one, other than the few nurses who spent extended periods of time with us, knew my sweet child still existed. One had to be in her presence more than a few moments to witness the strong essence emanating from our daughter. I adamantly believed my brave child remained mentally alert.

Almost two months had trickled by since Kim had been given anything by mouth. On one particularly warm afternoon in mid-April, I watched in awe as Betty squeezed a few drops of water from a syringe into Kim's mouth. Pulling the syringe away, the nurse commanded, "Kim, swallow for me please." Kim immediately obeyed.

"How did you know she could do that?" I asked in surprise.

"Well, when we changed her NG tube, she was able to swallow," Betty replied with a smile.

My thoughts immediately returned to the morning before Kim's first surgery when she lay dreaming of icy treats to soothe her parched mouth and throat. I remembered her plea, "Mom, can I have some green sherbet and a red ice pop?"

I relived my helplessness when I issued my tentative response: "Kimmie, when you are better, you can have anything you want. I promise sweetie."

Could I fulfill my promise now? I told Betty about my plan, and she quickly agreed. I raced down the stairs and through the corridors to the coffee shop. I couldn't give Kim the lime sherbet she requested, but I could offer her the next best thing.

When I returned to the room, three nurses were gathered around Kim in anticipation of the big event. Sarah adjusted the bed to elevate Kim's head, and May stood nearby with an emergency suctioning apparatus while Betty positioned herself opposite of me to help with any emergency.

I sat down on the bed. "Kimmie, I have a surprise for you. I brought you an ice pop. It's your favorite kind, red."

I unwrapped and separated the two frozen cherry treats, and discarded one before gently touching the second ice pop on a stick to Kim's lips. Her mouth was warm with fever. The tip of the treat instantly melted and deposited cool droplets of liquid into her parched mouth.

Fearfully, I begged, "Sweetie, swallow for me!"

Without hesitation, Kim took a large gulp, and everyone cheered in triumph. She not only swallowed those first few drops, but gradually consumed over half of the icy confection. I worried about giving her too much. Hesitant about pushing Kim beyond her abilities, I pulled the treat away. The muscles she used to swallow had not been utilized in months.

"Honey, do you want more?"

Slowly, she moved her head upward, then down to signal, "Yes."

Her response both thrilled and amazed us. The nurses cheered and applauded, while I wiped away tears just before touching the sweet treat once again to her lips.

Word of Kim's triumph spread rapidly throughout the hospital. When Dr. Carlton made his evening rounds, he immediately heard about the event. With lightning-quick strides, he stormed into our room, hastily examined Kim, and then pivoted toward me. "Is it true you gave *her* an ice pop today?"

When I confirmed the fact, he furiously rounded upon the nurses. "What would you have done if the patient had aspirated?"

He spun around, and stormed from the room while we stood in shocked silence.

I understood Dr. Carlton's position. His duty was to deliver uncompromised medical treatment to Kim, but a mother's heart soars beyond the medical and hovers over the cries of her child. By the gracious hand of God, Kim was able to swallow. Jesus stood in the room with us. His capable hand assisted me in fulfilling a promise I made months before. I could only praise my merciful Savior for his tender care.

CHAPTER 26 - GOD'S GRACE

Road of Grace, Salvation's Plan! Sent down from God to rescue man.

The weeks were passing quickly. Dr. Carlton extended Kim's radiation therapy from two weeks to four. She began to move her arms and legs, and I noted beginning signs of head movement. Nurses removed the Foley, and Kim's bladder functioned normally. I waited expectantly to catch a glimpse of her beautiful, blue eyes. On rare occasions a tiny flicker of a smile passed her lips, and love permeated the room.

One day Gina reappeared at our door. "My baby's back in the hospital with pneumonia this time. I asked Chad to stay with him for a few minutes so I could come and talk to you."

Her large, searching eyes bored into mine. "I haven't slept much in the past few weeks. I just can't get you or Kim out of my thoughts since we left the hospital. I keep thinking of the things you said to me the last time we spoke, and I know if anything like this ever happened to one of my children, I wouldn't be able to take it. I know I don't have what you have. It's like God is telling me I had better get right with him."

She paused briefly while absently twirling a lock of her hair before pressing on. "Before Chad and I were married, I converted from Catholicism to the Protestant faith. But since we got married, we hardly ever go to church. Sometimes we go on Easter and Christmas. Chad and I just don't know very much about the Bible, and we feel stupid and embarrassed every time we go."

"Father, help me," I silently pleaded. "I haven't truly witnessed to anyone since high school!"

"Gina," I replied, "It's just grace. None of us come to Jesus with a wealth of Bible knowledge; very few come with a long list of church attendance. People seek Jesus because they need something greater in their lives. They need God's love and peace. It's not about our worthiness; it's about accepting God's grace."

"I'm always hearing about grace, but I don't know what it means."

"It's God's free gift of mercy and pardon from sin that leads to eternal life. When we ask for his forgiveness, God pours his grace out upon us simply because he loves us. You can't earn it, or do anything to deserve grace; you just have to accept it in faith. Jesus paid the price for our sins in full by dying on the cross."

She trembled with frustration. "I still don't understand how grace works!"

I sighed, and looked upward. The room fell silent while Gina's glistening orbs stared at me, and I searched for words.

"This story isn't in the Bible; it's just how I've always imagined grace happening. I like to think God sent his angels to stand at the foot of the cross and collect every drop of blood that fell from Jesus as he was crucified.

"When we come to Jesus and ask to be forgiven, I picture God taking one of the vials from an angel and sprinkling drops of Christ's blood upon us. The blood trickles down upon our foreheads, and changes the way we think. It rolls across our hearts, washes away our sin, and leaves us with peace. Although we are still imperfect beings, God never sees our sins because Jesus' blood has blotted them out."

"But, what do I need to do?"

"What do you do when a friend knocks on your door?"

Puzzled, she answered, "Well, I open the door, and let her in."

"It's just as simple with Jesus too. When he knocks on the door of your heart, let him come in. The second you ask Jesus to come into your heart, he envelopes you in his love, and you are given the precious gifts of forgiveness and eternal life. Jesus establishes an everlasting relationship with you."

"But, I don't really know anything about Jesus!"

"When you place your trust in him, each of the things you are so worried about will fall into place. Jesus will fill all of the lonely spaces in your heart. You'll want to worship him and read his Word. Having Jesus in my heart is the only thing that enables me to get through this. When you surrender to Christ, you can survive the unthinkable because you are never alone."

Gina shook her head in silent dismay. She walked away with tears streaming from her eyes, and with the same haunting question on her mind: What would I do if that were my child?

At eight o'clock, I went downstairs to make my nightly phone call to Dan. Upon returning, I noticed a nurse standing in the doorway of our room speaking to Gina and her husband. As I approached, the three quickly dispersed.

Twenty minutes later, the same nurse returned and spoke to me in a hushed tone. "I found that couple standing in your room. I thought you might not want people staring at your daughter, so I asked them to leave."

Following her exit, I slipped from the room and headed toward the east wing in search of Gina and Chad. I stopped midway when I noticed the couple standing near the elevator. They appeared to be upset and deeply involved in a conversation, so I decided against discussing the incident with them. I sensed an unease about Gina, but not wanting to interfere in something which may not have concerned me, I said a quick prayer for her, returned to our room, and drifted off to sleep.

The following morning, Gina burst into our room. "You'll never guess what happened!"

"Probably not. What happened?"

"Well, last night Chad and I were standing outside Kim's room. We were just watching her, but the nurse told us to leave. I'm sorry if we did something wrong. We think she's the most beautiful child we have ever seen. Both of us want a little girl to complete our family, and if we are ever blessed with one, we want her to be just like Kim."

I could only reply with a tearful nod. I also wanted a little girl just like Kim. Please God; let it happen!

"Marie," we weren't just staring at Kim. God was drawing us to her; we couldn't leave. Chad and I were so scared. We knew if anything like this ever happened to one of our kids, we couldn't handle it."

"Gina, I—"

"Wait! I need to tell you this. Last night when Chad left the hospital, he was really upset. All he could think about was Kim and our two boys. He was in such a daze that he didn't pay any attention to where he was going. He just drove down one street after another until he realized he was lost. He finally pulled the car into a parking lot and stayed there until he felt calm enough to drive home. But... this is the amazing part! At midnight, he came back to the hospital, and he walked into our room carrying a Bible."

My brows shot upward in a bewildered look.

She smiled infectiously. "I haven't seen Chad read the Bible since we got married. But when he finally got home last night, he hunted until he found one in the closet. He said he needed to find some answers."

"What kind of answers?"

"Where's—?" Gina whipped around, scanning the room. "Oh, never mind. I see it." She strode with purpose toward the window and retrieved my Bible from the ledge. "Give me a minute, and I'll show you what I mean."

She thumbed through the pages until she found the correct verse. "Chad was really upset and agitated. When he found our Bible, he opened it up, and this was the first verse he saw." Pointing to the scripture while handing me the Bible, she commanded, "Read this."

I zeroed in on the words, "Come unto me, all ye that labour and are heavy laden, and I will give you rest" (Matt. 11:28 KJV).

Tears welled in my eyes. "God has a way of leading us to the exact words we need to hear."

"Well, that's not the only one he found. The next scripture he came across really got to him, and he couldn't wait to come back here to show it to me." She took the Bible and once more scanned page by page until she located the second verse. "Here, read this one."

I took the sacred book and read its words. "Jesus saith unto him, I am the way, the truth, and the life: no man cometh unto the Father, but by me" (John 14:6).

Gina wore a look of pure joy when she exclaimed, "Last night, when I read those passages out loud, God spoke to us. Chad and I got down on our knees and prayed. I said, 'Jesus, if you are real, then come into my life, and just let me feel you!' Those words were barely out of my mouth when I felt something touch me, and I trembled all over!"

Tears clouded my vision, and muffled my voice. "How wonderful," I whispered. "I'm so happy for you and Chad."

"There's more! When I asked Jesus to forgive me, everything happened just like you said it would. He came into my heart, and took away all of my guilt and worries. I don't understand it, but somehow they were just instantly gone!"

Tears poured from her eyes when Gina softly added, "Now I have a peace I can't explain."

What words can I add to her testimony? Had there been no others touched by God through our small child, the testimony given by Gina is enough to prove God's hand placed every perfect piece of his plan together. Jesus used our precious Kim to reach out to others while his spirit began to touch their hearts. God amazed me with his ability to use a beautiful child, lying peacefully still in a hospital bed, to draw the lost unto him.

> *"That if thou shalt confess with thy mouth the Lord Jesus, and shalt believe in thine heart that God hath raised him from the dead, thou shalt be saved"(Rom.10:9).*

Over the following days, Gina dropped by each afternoon, and we immersed ourselves in long conversations about the certainty of God's love, and his all-sustaining peace. Our talks gave me added strength as I shared my favorite scriptures with her.

One night she tapped on our door, and asked to speak with me. Because I sensed the seriousness of the conversation, and believed her thoughts were centered on my child's illness, I suggested, "Let's go across the hall to the Parent's Room so we can speak privately. I need to tell a nurse where I'm going, and then I'll meet you there."

I informed the charge nurse where I would be and why. At the news, the nurse bluntly asked, "Don't you have enough to worry about without taking all of the world's problems on your shoulders?"

I could never claim to be a self-sacrificing person; but when the nurse voiced her opinion, I immediately realized this was exactly God's purpose for me. I lived in a hospital—separated from my family and friends. I had no responsibilities other than to love Kim and oversee her needs. My parents were caring for my other children, and Dan lived alone. What else could I do? The Lord planted me here. If someone needed help finding the truth about Jesus, then this was his plan for me.

Gina nervously paced the room. When I entered from the hallway, she blurted, "I just don't understand it! Why would a loving God allow a thing like this to happen?"

She asked the same question I stumbled over every day. Her quandary forced me to directly face the situation in order to supply an answer.

"First of all Gina, I want you to understand one thing. God never seeks to destroy anyone. He loves us with a passion we can't comprehend. However, I believe he sometimes allows things for a greater purpose."

She shook her head in disbelief. "I don't understand. What kind of purpose?"

"I don't have all the answers yet; I'm not that wise. I'm just taking things day by day."

"I can't think of any good answer or reason for this!"

"Well, I've witnessed countless spiritual transformations because of Kim's illness. Nurses, friends, and perfect strangers have been touched and forever changed because God placed us in this hospital. It's about souls. I'm not the only person in the world who is hurting. I understand that more every day."

"But is it worth all the heartache you're going through?"

"Sometimes it would be so easy to throw up my hands and say, 'God, I quit! I don't want to do this! Just stop the world from spinning and let me off!'"

"That's what I want to know Marie. What keeps you from saying those very words?"

"Reality hits, and I understand it's God who helps me get up each morning to face another day. In those tender moments when I am totally dependent upon him, I feel more love than I've ever experienced before. It's as if God is so close I can reach out and touch him, and I know he's holding my hand."

She shook her head incredulously, "But ... is it really worth it?"

Glancing briefly toward the hallway, I answered. "These words keep running through my mind: Who is able to judge what God considers one soul to be worth?"

Her tear-filled eyes stared directly into mine. I grasped her hand. "Gina, Kim's illness brought you and Chad to the Lord. Her beauty, along with the cancer, drew you to her and made you see how fragile life is. Kim helped you realize how much you needed Jesus in your life. Don't question how he does things or why. You are one of the reasons."

"But doesn't God know how much this is hurting you?"

"He knows all too well. At first, I screamed, 'Lord, you don't know how much this hurts!'"

"He answered, 'I Gave My Son Also.' God watched as his son was beaten, cursed, spit upon, and crucified. Yes, Gina, he knows exactly how I feel."

Persistently, she came back at me, "How will you stand it if Kim dies?"

"I don't know. Trusting God is one of the most difficult things we are called to do. It means believing he has a reason and a plan for every ripple or occurrence in our lives. He sent his son to die for us. Seeing my own child lying in a hospital bed makes me realize exactly how great his sacrifice was. If death happens, I pray God's strength will be greater than my pain."

"I don't think I could ever be as strong as you."

"Gina, do you really think I'm strong? I am scared to death every minute of the day and night. But unfortunately, I can't make this go away. I don't have any other choice than to push through it minute by minute."

"If I were you, I'd be begging God every second."

"I can't just ask for Kim's life if that's all I will have. She could linger in her present state for years to come. I don't want *existence* for my child; I want laughter, running and playing, along with kisses and hugs. I can only ask God to do what is best for Kim."

She shook her head in dismay, "I still don't see how you will do it."

"This is the only thing I know for certain: God has sustained me through all of these weeks, and he will not leave me—even if the worst happens."

Gina's pounding at me culminated with her final question. "Do you believe in miracles?"

At last, I could relax and smile. "Yes! Some may call me a fool to believe in miracles, but if it's foolish to believe God can heal, then I am happy to be a fool. The doctor gave us no hope when Kim lay in a coma, but now she is waking up! God has brought her this far for a reason, and I am still praying for a miracle."

"You know," she replied. "I can't help thinking Kim's miracle is very near."

We hugged one another as I confessed, "I think so too."

Our conversation ended, and I slipped quietly back into my sleeping child's room to gaze once more upon her beautiful face.

Kim became a little more alert each day. She began to move her head toward voices, and she was gaining more motor control. We had no way to gage just how much she understood, but on occasion, I saw glimpses of her former self.

I cherish the moment when I leaned close to her precious face and whispered, "I can't wait for the time when your sweet arms can hug my neck once again."

Without hesitation, her arms began to deliberately move upward in an attempt to touch me. I eased her struggle by gently lifting her arms and placing those precious hands upon my shoulders. I held her in my arms for an embrace; Kim's tiny fingers squeezed tightly into my neck as she tried to hold on.

It was such a sweet moment, but I never uttered those words again. I understood with clarity how heartbreaking and confusing it was for her to be unable to show the love she once so freely gave.

Each new dawn became brighter and filled with more promise. Kim's beautiful blue eyes drew me into her soul once again. The tumor may have impaired her motor skills, but no one could ever convince me it had diminished my daughter's essence. I sensed her indomitable spirit in every waking moment.

Gina came to visit once more before her baby was released. "I'm really sorry Kim hasn't been healed. I truly believed God would perform his miracle before we left the hospital. Why do you think it hasn't happened? I don't understand why God hasn't answered our prayers."

"I don't know why Kim hasn't been completely healed yet, but one miracle has already taken place. You and Chad found Jesus; his love will never leave you."

Gina lowered her head. "I have a confession to make. I've told all of my friends about your sweet little girl. One of those friends, Carrie, came to the hospital and asked me to take her to see Kim. You were downstairs in the chapel, so we walked in here without permission."

"It's okay. I trust you."

She nodded in agreement. "There's something you need to know. Carrie has a little boy about the same age as Kim, but from the day he was born, she's refused to love or accept him in any way. She just never wanted a child."

"Oh how sad! That poor little boy has never known a mother's love."

"But, here's the good thing. Something came over Carrie when she walked into this room. She imagined her son lying there in that bed instead of Kim, and she began to cry so hard I thought she would never stop. I can't believe it, but after all these years she finally realized God had placed a precious life in her hands, and she had rejected his gift."

I trembled. God's omniscient power claimed victory over the indifference and resentment shown toward the least of his innocent children. He was reshaping and molding others into his image before our very eyes!

"Gina, do you remember asking me why God would allow a child to suffer? Don't you see how God is moving and working not only in your life, but in the lives of others all around you? He changed your life as well as Chad's, and now your friend has been changed."

She smiled with sudden understanding. "I've been thinking about something else too. I think it was God's plan to put our baby in the hospital. The first time Brendon was admitted, his temperature returned to normal within hours. They never found out why he had a fever spike, but that's when I saw you and Kim through the window. I think the only possible explanation for the temperature swing is because God wanted us to come in contact with Kim."

I agreed. From the very beginning, Gina was spiritually drawn toward finding peace with God. During their second stay in the hospital, both she and Chad kneeled before Jesus and asked him to come into their hearts and lives.

"And we know that all things work together for good to them that love God, to them who are called according to his purpose" (Rom. 8:28).

Chapter 27 - The Swirling Storm

The peace we receive from God does not necessarily mean the problems we face will be immediately removed. A struggle is not about making the problem disappear. It's about the companion we choose to walk beside us through the problem. Jesus supremely reigns as the best choice.

Kim and I were on an uphill journey. The mountain upon which we were climbing was steep, but with Kim making such great progress, I believed we could easily reach the pinnacle. Sadly, within days of Gina's departure, Kim's upward stride came to a sudden halt. She began a slow, backward descent upon the rocky slope, and I could neither prevent nor break her fall. Daily improvements vanished. Kim moved her limbs less frequently. We waited daily for new signs of progress in Kim's battle, but few came. Tensions mounted.

My fears increased further when Dr. Carlton remarked, "Kim doesn't exhibit as much movement as before. In fact, I haven't observed any improvement recently."

I used this opportunity to ask my most troubling questions. "Does this mean the treatments have reached their peak? Will Kim remain like this forever?"

His reply varied little from those in the past. "I can't give you definite answers when dealing with the brain. Kim might remain in this state, or she could continue waking up. This process could last anywhere from a few months to a year."

I summoned the courage to address my greatest fear. "If Kim wakes up completely within the year, will she be healed, or could the tumor come back?"

Dr. Carlton answered methodically, and in a tone parents use when reasoning with a small child. "Radiation never destroys; it simply shrinks the tumor."

My heart fell to my stomach. There had never been any medical hope for Kim. We only borrowed a little more time. Had my heart once again tuned out the unbearable?

As soon as possible, I scuttled across the room, ran down the stairs, and exited the hospital. My feet carried me around the block. Each step became more deliberate as I attempted to stomp out the bitterness and resentment welling up inside.

A strong, southwest wind blew across the area. Sand whirled in the air. The blustery storm pushed against me. I ducked my head and kept trudging against the force of the gale. The wind symbolized everything raging inside of me. I pushed back against death, separation and heartache.

The wind roared. Its deafening sound afforded me the opportunity to scream aloud my protests. "I'm here Lord! Where are you? Don't you see me? Don't you hear me? Do you care? I'm here Lord! Lord, I'm here!"

The gusts of wind grew stronger. Dust and debris pelted my face, making it impossible to breathe. Its thrust forced me to turn back and seek shelter. When I approached the doors of the hospital's entrance, I looked up toward heaven. The bright sun burned through the haze of swirling sand, sending out brilliant streaks of red and blue across the sky. Only God could create such beauty in the midst of a swirling storm.

The warmth of God's love permeated my stricken soul. The

wind whipped around me; sand whirled around in funnels on the sidewalk, but I felt none of it. His perfect peace cocooned me.

Why am I worried? Nothing's changed. Dr. Carlton suggested radiation only as a means of doing everything possible to save Kim. The doctors in the best cancer treatment center in Texas advised against radiation. They believed Kim's brain had sustained too much damage to benefit from the therapy.

Kim's fate never rested in the hands of physicians. This fact was proved when the doctors discovered the tumor in the very center of her brain ... the one place impossible to surgically reach ... either to diagnose or to remove. No, from the very beginning, Kim's life was firmly planted in God's hands. God could still heal; cancer was not greater than my heavenly Father!

Jesus' presence on the day of the storm gave me the courage to face whatever lay ahead, but the following weeks were difficult at best. Kim's series of treatments were completed. Doctors released Timmy, the young leukemia patient, and his leaving made me yearn for Dirk and Kristi even more. Additionally, no other inquisitive visitors entered our world. My life became a series of lonely days and miserable nights.

Friends and nurses were faithful, but God's movement among the lives of others had become one of my greatest sources of strength. I equated Kim's health and well-being with the endless stream of souls needing a special touch of Christ's love, but one day after another trickled by without new faces or visitors.

Doubts assailed. An inner voice whispered, "You've been deserted."

My heart rejected any such thought. I believed with certainty we were not alone on this treacherous slope. Jesus richly supplied us with caring nurses who walked with us each step of the way. From the onset of the coma, the nurses attending Kim dutifully prepared me for what lay ahead. The picture they painted of Kim's future looked dark and bleak.

"Most cancer patients with this type of tumor will develop noticeable symptoms. Kim may experience tremors and abnormal posturing. Her limbs may become rigid and atrophied. Kim's muscle tone will deteriorate, causing the corners of her mouth to droop and drool. She may not be able to hear or have any vision."

Much to the nurses' astonishment, the list of Kim's physical maladies thus far was minor. The glory of the Lord surrounded her. She lingered as a sleeping princess.

Surely this means when every heart in God's plan is reached, Kim will be healed without any lasting physical effects!

CHAPTER 28 - STRENGTH IN THE NIGHT

Time endlessly dragged on. One day was much like the other. I spent the hours rocking Kim, pressing her sweet body close to mine, and expressing my love for her. Only her soft breaths, and the rattle of trays in the hall, broke the silence.

The nights were unending. Sleep did not come, so I stood at the window and peered into the darkness. In those long, gloomy hours, I allowed myself to cry for the lost moments with my family. I could only trust that one day my other children would understand what a difficult choice it had been to leave them behind while I took care of Kim. Our stay was meant to be temporary. We hoped Kim might be released and on her way to recovery within two weeks of the surgery. Those few weeks evolved into six weeks, and now we were exceeding two months.

Dan drove up each Wednesday night for a short visit. His presence gave me the courage to keep going until we saw one another again on Saturday. Weekend visits with my family became the highlight of each week. The medical staff turned a blind eye to the visitors who streamed into the hallway each Sunday afternoon. Among those visitors were a six-year-old boy and a two-month-old baby. I immediately sensed when they entered the hallway. The air pulsated with a sudden surge of energy in an otherwise sterile environment.

Dad appeared at the door first; he bent down to kiss his precious granddaughter then held Kimmie's hand while tears dripped from his eyes. I quickly walked to the corridor where I fell on my knees to embrace my son. Mother sat in the corner of the waiting room holding Kristi. Not long afterward, Dan's parents joined us. I spent those few precious hours soaking in the essence of my family, laughing at Dirk's adventures, and cuddling my infant while each family member took turns visiting alone with Kim.

Seemingly before it had begun, the day ended, and my family lined up for goodbye hugs before walking down the steps. Dan lingered behind a moment longer to wrap me in his arms before catching up with the others. I watched behind the glass doors until they were out of sight, then turned to walk alone down the long stretch of hallway and back to the stillness. Loneliness enveloped me in the hours following their visit. Sleep inevitably alluded me on those nights.

In the hushed hours between midnight and dawn, I stood at the window, peered into the darkness, and yearned for the happiness we once shared. I needed my husband beside me to give me courage for the continuous battle raging in my heart, but the medical bills were mounting. Dan committed himself to long hours of work to keep up with all the extra expenses incurred through our hospital stay.

I sensed the heavy toll my absence placed upon each family member. Mother and Dad were exhausted. Dirk distanced himself from me to guard his heart. He now believed his home was with my parents; I was the person he visited.

Kristi fussed in my arms; Mother and Dad were the only parents she recognized. The voice my infant heard singing to her in the womb no longer existed in her memory. I missed the important time of bonding with my newborn, and now in the midst of darkness, I worried about losing each of my children.

More often than not, an eerie silence pulled me abruptly from these thoughts. *Has Kim stopped breathing?*

Each time I ran to her bed, and leaned my head close to hers in search of a puff of air to confirm she was still with me. When I could not feel a breath, I placed my hand upon her chest as a sickening dread engulfed my heart.

"No, Kim, no! It's not time for you to leave me!" I inwardly gasped, and as if on cue, I felt a slight flutter beneath my hand.

These were my nights. I spent countless hours filled with the fear of losing one child in death, and the fear of losing my other children in the aftermath. Yet in those dark hours, I saw no other choice. Kim could not be left alone. Friends and family routinely offered to help, but I could not bring myself to leave her again.

A ninety minute drive to our home was simply too far away. Dan and I were the only ones who could give written consent for any life-saving measures. The early morning phone call we received from Dr. Carlton following Kim's first surgery, pounded this vital fact into our inexperienced thinking. I needed to be readily available in case of an emergency. In the agonizing darkness, I depended upon my Savior to wrap his arms around me.

On Friday, the twenty-sixth day of April, Dr. Carlton made subtle hints about finding a good nursing home. I expected him to press me for a decision very soon. On the following Monday, fear and depression engulfed me. I sensed something ominous lying in wait. Has God forgotten us?

At noon, I sat beside Kim quietly asking God to give me a sign of his presence. "Lord, it's been so long since you've sent anyone our way. If there are no more souls to be reached, then why haven't you healed Kim? The treatments are over, and the doctor wants to dismiss her soon. Please work quickly Lord; heal her before we leave. I will never willingly commit Kimmie to a nursing home. Father, I need you. Please help me Lord; just let me know something!"

Within minutes of my prayer, a man, wearing boots, a white western shirt, and crisply starched jeans, knocked on the door before stepping into the room. He nervously twirled his cowboy hat in his hands while addressing me.

"Pardon me ma'am. Is this Kimberly Grissom's room?"

Believing his sudden appearance meant another curiosity seeker, I answered him with a frosty, "Yes."

Despite my less than friendly reception, he walked over to the bed, held out his hand to shake mine, and introduced himself as Bill, an old friend of Dan's.

"I've heard about your little girl, and I'm sorry she's been so sick. Would you mind if I prayed for her?"

Delightedly surprised, I answered, "I would very much appreciate your prayer."

As I bowed my head, God's presence immediately drenched my soul. A mere stranger stood at my child's side pleading with God to heal her, to shelter Kim in his arms, and to take care of her every need. I was amazed by this man's ability to grasp the concerns of my heart, and to convey those feelings to the Lord. His prayer could have only been directed by the Holy Spirit.

Following his prayer, Bill described how he was compelled to come to the hospital. "I've had this child on my mind day and night for weeks. I've prayed for her over and over at home, but God wanted me to come and pray beside Kim today. I tried to ignore him. I said, 'I don't have time right now; I'll stop by on my way home tonight.'

"But when I was driving by this big ole building a few

minutes ago, I heard the Lord say, 'You don't need lunch, but there's a little girl inside that hospital who needs your prayers!' I didn't have a choice; God wouldn't leave me alone until I parked my truck and walked in here."

I stood in awe of God's power as it swept across us, and moved others in the direction he desired, just to bring comfort to a helpless mother and her child.

Before leaving, Bill tenderly clasped Kim's hand and boldly stated, "I feel good about her. I know everything will be all right."

I could only smile in agreement. Yes, I felt good about her too. For the first time in days, I experienced peace because my heavenly Father had not forgotten us. I pondered the moment; this was an unparalleled visit from God who orchestrates each kind word and act of mercy. A total stranger spoke the exact words the Holy Spirit had whispered to me countless times, "Everything is all right."

CHAPTER 29 - PRONOUNCED GUILTY

The inevitable happened. The day I feared for weeks arrived. Doctor Carlton stood in Kim's room pressing me for a decision about placing my daughter in a nursing facility. Thinking Kim might be better in a few weeks, I asked for more time.

With his patience nearing an end, the doctor chose his words with precision. "She's been here for months with little change. There could be many more months without improvement, or death could occur at any time."

"I understand the things you are telling me, but I—"

"The sooner you accept the fact, the better off you will be. Right now, Kim only needs good nursing supervision and care. She doesn't *need* a mother, but your other children do, and your husband needs a wife!"

My stomach slammed against my spine as though I had been kicked. Willing myself to stay calm until the doctor exited the room, I pushed back the mounting panic rising inside of me by digging my nails into the palms of my hands.

The doctor stared in my direction, and waited for a response. When none was forthcoming, he pivoted on his heels, and stormed from the room in exasperation.

I turned my attention from the door, and focused on the sunlight flooding through the window. Had he meant to hurt me in such a cruel manner?

Anger bubbled up as my soul soundlessly seethed. My child is no stuffed doll! This is the same child who once ran to me with outstretched arms and whispered, "Mom, I love you," while planting gentle kisses on my cheek.

Although the tumor is robbing her body of any movement and muting her ability to speak, Kim's spirit endures. She recognizes my voice! I am absolutely certain she understands the things I say. Each time I hold her, I feel her body respond to my touch. How can I just abandon her in some facility, forget Kim ever existed, and return to my other children?

What reason could I ever give Dirk and Kristi to explain why I left their sister in an institution to die alone? I will fight with my last breath against it!

I looked toward my precious child lying on the bed of white. Her eyes were rapidly darting back and forth in search of me. I bolted across the room. Using one hand to support her head and fragile neck, while lifting her body with the other, I cradled Kim in my arms and carried her to the rocking chair.

"Don't worry sweetie; Mommy's right here. I will never leave you. When we leave here, we will go home so you can be with Daddy, Dirk and the baby every day. It's okay Kimmie; just relax and go to sleep. Mom's here. I love you baby; I will never leave you."

Before long, her eyes closed in sleep, and I permitted myself to reconsider the physician's words. I could no longer block them out. Maybe he was right. Perhaps she did not need me, but oh, how I needed Kim! I needed to be with her for as long as she lived. I needed to touch her; I needed to hold and comfort her. I needed to feel those taunt muscles relax in my arms. I needed to know I could do something to make her death easier.

The nurses returned shortly after Dr. Carlton left the pediatric floor. They gathered in the doorway of our room, and waited for me to speak. I said nothing until I placed Kim safely on the bed and properly supported her body with pillows.

I stepped away from the bed, and exhaled a long, shuddering breath before tearfully shrieking, "Is he right? Does she not need me? Is she not aware of my presence?"

The nurses fell into the room, and surrounded me in a group embrace.

May soothed, "We don't think the doctor meant the words like they sounded. He was merely trying to prepare you for Kim's death. He only meant you need to be with the other members of your family."

Liz spoke up. "Your family needs you, and you need your family. If anything happens to Kim, your family might not be able to make it here in time. You would be here alone."

Betty summed up everyone's opinion. "There is nothing you can really do for her right now other than give her your love. And yes, of course she needs her mother!"

In spite of the nurses' kind efforts, Dr. Carlton's scornful words chipped away at my heart and threatened to shatter it. Oh dear God how could he think she needs nothing other than a bed and a place to die? Every human being needs love; without love we can't exist! I am with Kim each hour of the day. I know she is still with me in mind and spirit. She may die, but she will not die without love!

Nevertheless, my stubborn vow of devotion to Kim plunged me head first into a dark chasm where I dwelled upon every aspect of my worst fears. Each moment of the day I carried the guilt of abandoning her both before and after the surgeries. Additionally, I bore the guilt of being absent from the lives of my other children. This must be what everyone is thinking— that I blithely gave up Dirk and Kristi to be with Kim!

I secretly spent each night crying for my son and infant.

Dirk's life was turned upside down. He lost his sister and best friend overnight. Everything he had ever known was suddenly ripped from him, and from the beginning, he sensed our lives would never be the same. My newborn recognized her grandmother, but not her mother. I watched helplessly time after time as Kristi smiled when Mother took her from my arms.

Shaking with anger, I obsessed over every bitter word Dr. Carlton spewed at me. His words echoed in my brain. "Kim doesn't need a mother! Your other children do."

"OOH!" I gasped in sudden horror. Like words on a blinking billboard, the truth flashed before me. I was no different from the other mothers I railed against so vehemently! I abandoned two of my three children and failed to offer them the comfort and nurturing they needed to survive. My parents were supplying their needs while I ensconced myself in this hospital room stubbornly holding on to my other child. Why had I not recognized my miserable failure before?

Given a choice only the Wisdom of Solomon could decide, I was not wise enough to grasp the answer. I only knew I must fight for Kimmie's life, and make up for all of those days when I could not be beside her. I could only hope I would have the rest of my life to prove to my other children how much they were loved.

Guilt taunted and screamed at me. The mingled thoughts simply became too much to bear. I knew of only one safe haven. I quietly walked down the dark flight of stairs and entered the hospital chapel to seek solace. This time there were no outcries, no pleas for mercy. I sought solitude in order to hear the voice of my Master.

In the stillness of the beautifully ornate room, I realized the nurses were right. Doctor Carlton's words were aimed toward jolting me into reality. He tried everything to make me understand the seriousness of Kim's situation. He viewed the outcome as dire, and he alone held the responsibility to make me understand the circumstances.

Although his words were painful, I'm grateful he never gave us false hope. But no matter what anyone said, my hope was based on something more powerful than medicine. My trust was centered in Jesus Christ, who could do all things— including the impossible.

After considering the few options available to us, Dan and I decided to transfer Kim back to our local hospital. Once we were home, we could enlist Dr. Paul and our families to help us make the best decision. But the actual transfer was delayed for an indefinite period of time. Kim's elevated temperature persisted, and tests must be performed to determine the cause.

Dr. Carlton stated, "I won't transfer Kim with an infection; we'll need to perform recommended treatments first." Tests revealed a few mild infections which were treated and resolved quickly, but Kim's elevated temperature continued to hover consistently at one hundred and one degrees.

CHAPTER 30 - OUR HOPE RESTS IN JESUS

Seemingly overnight, Kim began to choke after each feeding. Her weakened system could no longer digest food in the normal amount of time, thus making it impossible for tube feedings to be administered consistently every two hours. Kim often missed four of the eight prescribed feedings per day. Severe pain accompanied each breath she took.

Nurses began turning Kim's frail body every half-hour. I watched her teeth clench, and her hands double into fists as she wrestled with the pain. She could not indicate the location of her discomfort; we assumed it radiated from her head and neck. This, we believed, might only be a reaction to the radiation.

My world was crumbling around me. I yearned for privacy—a place to weep and pray until I found peace—but no avenue for solace existed. Too many others sought sanctuary in the chapel throughout the day, and by late afternoon, its doors were closed. My concerns about Kim's condition made me fear leaving the hospital.

Throughout those long nights, when I could not find a closet for prayer, I reached for my Bible and silently read the book of Psalms. Each psalm became a prayer, an outcry for help, and a pleading for mercy. One night out of desperation, I penned a prayer from my heart to God:

Lord Jesus, when I doubt, hold me in your keeping.
When I stumble, pick me up. Plant my feet in
faith—not in what is seen—but in your unending
mercy and love. Stiffen my spine to walk in belief
toward thy throne, where prayers are answered.
When others around me doubt, let me bravely cry,
"Believe, and it shall be done!" Can I hide my fear
and trembling from you O God? Can I sway my
own doubts? Nay, I will tremble in my unbelief and
say, "My God is greater than my fear!"

Pam completed her rotation on another floor, and was back in charge of the midnight shift in Pediatrics. Periodically, she entered our room, pulled up a stool, and sat down to answer each of my medical queries. Other nurses gave me guarded information, so I depended upon her to give me the unvarnished truth. The honesty she provided helped prepare me for the days ahead.

On one occasion, shortly after two in the morning, Pam slipped quietly into the room. A muted light over the bed silhouetted Kim's image in an otherwise dark space. I didn't speak. I thought she came in only to make a quick check on Kim before returning to her other duties. Instead, she sat down on a stool beside the bed and leaned over the rail to lovingly touch my daughter. Her hand softly stroked Kim's cheek and forehead. I lay on the pull-out bed without moving. I couldn't bring myself to intrude upon such a poignant moment.

From the darkened stillness, Pam exhaled a deep sigh. Thinking the hands of death had quietly snatched my child, I leaped up, and instantaneously covered the distance between our two beds. My eyes rapidly scanned the scene. Kim was breathing!

"Pam, what's wrong?"

She quickly straightened her spine. "Everything's fine; I was just thinking of the past. My baby would be due about now. Do you remember me telling you about my miscarriage?"

"Yes, I remember. I've thought of talking to you about it so often, but I didn't know how to bring up the subject."

"It's not something I wanted to talk about. I wouldn't have allowed you to bring it up anyway."

Avoiding my eyes, she lowered her head. "Tom and I thought we just couldn't handle it financially. The last thing we needed was another mouth to feed. Then, a few weeks later, I had a miscarriage."

"I'm so sorry."

Lifting her chin, she focused her gaze upon Kim. "I haven't been able to shake my guilt since then. I thought God took my baby to punish me for not wanting it."

Thinking about my own guilt, I chose not to speak.

Pam caressed Kim's hand. "This child is so beautiful. I've never heard her speak, but I can tell she was the sweetest little girl anyone could ever hope to have. I just realized how much God loves her. There's no way He would use this child to hurt you. And if God loves her, then he loved my baby too."

"God knew you would love your baby, and he sees your heartache too. Let me get my Bible; I want to read you some verses that helped me."

I held God's Word in the shadow of light above my child. "The Lord is compassionate and gracious, slow to anger, abounding in love. ... he does not treat us as our sins deserve or repay us according to our iniquities. For as high as the heavens are above the earth, so great is his love for those who fear him; as far as the east is from the west, so far has he removed our transgressions from us" (Ps.103:8, 10—12 NIV).

Pam solemnly moved her head from side to side in dismay. "I see so many sick kids every day. I don't think I'll ever understand why children have to die."

"Our eyes can't always see the good things that come from our heartaches; it just hurts too much. But when I focus on the blessings instead of my pain, I am comforted by his goodness. One thing's for certain; we've both been brought closer to God through our children. Whether we've failed him or sinned against him ... God's love supersedes our mess-ups, and he has us exactly where he wants us to be ... close to him."

Leaving me to ponder the moment, Pam smiled and returned to her station. I marveled over God's strategic planning. Our omnipotent Lord looked down upon this small area of the earth, and directed each hurting soul toward a tiny little girl lying in a hospital bed. It's astounding how the silence of a child can roar so profoundly.

CHAPTER 31 - THE UNRAVELING

The seams of our lives were coming unraveled one thread at a time. Another week passed without Kim's transfer. Her temperature rose to one hundred and two degrees without a definitive cause. The choking persisted. On Friday, Dr. Carlton suspected pneumonia and ordered X-rays.

While we were in the X-ray lab, Dr. Kincaid remarked about the noticeable changes in Kim since his last visit. "She is more alert, and motor control is improved. Her muscle tone is improving as well."

"So, do you think this means there's a possibility she will get better?" I inquired.

"Yes, there is still hope for her; the spike in temperature might be only a lingering effect of the radiation." Dr. Kincaid stroked Kim's forehead. "Time can make a difference as the brain tissue heals."

On Saturday morning, Dr. Carlton emerged from the nurses' station with Kim's lab reports in his hand. "Each of the tests proved negative for any infection, and there are no known causes for the fever. I see no reason to delay her transfer beyond next week."

Dan arrived shortly afterward. He gathered me into his arms and whispered, "I love you. We'll find a way to get through this."

On Sunday, our families came to visit, and to lend us strength and support. Seeing Dirk and Kristi gave me new resolve to fight for each of my children. When the time arrived for everyone to leave, and after all the goodbyes were said, I walked down the familiar hallway to our room.

Two nurses were hovering over Kim. One was using a syringe attached to the feeding tube to extract fluid from Kim's stomach. Becoming more alarmed by the minute, I watched as the two took turns drawing syringe after syringe filled with a dark green substance. They extracted a greater amount of fluid than Kim had been fed all day. She lay pale, and obviously in pain.

The night wore endlessly on. I anxiously paced the room with waves of panic surging through me. I didn't know what was wrong, but this was something significant.

"Oh Kim, why does something else go wrong every time you get better?"

Watching her suffer while lying in such agony seared my heart; nevertheless, I prayed my selfish prayer. "No Lord! No! I can't give her up!"

Among all the pleas I offered daily on Kim's behalf, one petition stood out among the rest: "Father, if she can't be healed, please help her speak the words, 'I love you.' I just want to hear her sweet voice once more.

"If not for me Lord, then please allow it for Kimmie. Her short life has been devoted to professing her love. For Kim's sake, please find a way for her to express what is in her heart! Lord, she called for me over and over, and I wasn't here to answer. Please give me the privilege of hearing her voice so I can answer when she calls."

Within the depths of my soul, I was certain God would grant me this request. I hid it away in my heart. If I told others, they might think I had stepped over the edge of sanity. Many believed it already.

They shake their heads in pity while asking, "Why do you continue to talk and sing to her? She can't hear you."

I allow each chastising word to wash across my heart. Let them pity me. My child is still with me!

Kim's eyes had not closed in almost twenty-four hours. Her pain persistently increased, and nurses kept a careful watch on her throughout the night. Shortly before six o'clock in the morning, the charge nurse returned and asked me to leave the room for a few moments. "I've called the doctor," she explained. "Kim's bladder has ceased to function."

The hands of death were reaching in to steal our daughter one piece at a time. Which nightmare might follow this? I expected either hemorrhaging of the brain or a coma. I helplessly watched Kim's life ebbing away.

While waiting, I picked up the receiver from the phone in the hallway, and dialed the person I needed.

"Dan, Kim is worse."

"Hold on Babe," he replied. "I'll be there in a little while. I love you."

Before stepping back into the room, I prayed, "Lord, my life is disintegrating, and I need you to help me!"

Pam stood beside Kim; she spoke softly while stroking my daughter's hand. "I'll be praying for you."

It was God's perfect timing. Pam sat with me on our first night of sorrow, and her strength would fortify me again today.

Sensing I might have only hours, or minutes, left with my child, I pulled up a stool and sat beside Kimmie. She could slip into a coma at any time, and never again hear my voice. So many thoughts welled up inside of me, yet I didn't possess the words to adequately express my emotions. I resorted to the only way I knew to convey our love to her.

"Kim, I love you. And Daddy loves you. And honey, Dirkie and the baby love you. And Granny and Pawpaw, and Grandma and Grandpa love you. And Missy loves you. And Kimmie, Jesus loves you too."

My arms longed to bestow caresses, but Kim's pain had increased dramatically. Dr. Carlton advised against moving her any more than necessary. Nurses limited me to holding her only once per day while the linens on the bed were changed. Unfortunately, the bed was no larger than a small crib, so instead of lying beside her, or holding her tightly in my arms, I sat holding Kim's clenched fists and kissing her gently.

Within two hours of my call, Dan arrived. "I should have stayed here with you last night instead of going home. I knew something was wrong."

He fought to be strong for my sake, but his deep set eyes projected the sorrow in his heart. Moments later, the doctor arrived to examine Kim. Her abdomen was distended, and slight tremors were developing throughout her body.

Dr. Carlton spoke directly to Dan. "Your daughter's condition has definitely deteriorated. I foresee no hope for improvement. Our best recourse at this time is to transfer her within a few days, and get both your daughter and wife home as soon as possible."

His meaning was clear. The tumor must again be growing. The disease could also be spreading throughout her body as evidenced by the difficulty she experienced with digestion, and the increased swelling of her stomach.

Kim lay in sheer agony after the doctor's palpation of her abdomen.

A nurse informed us, "I'm sorry; nothing can be done to relieve the pain."

Refusing to look me in the eye, she stared down at the floor, and quickly exited the room.

Dan drew his right hand into a fist and plunged it into his left palm. "I'd like to punch my fist through this wall!"

"You want to fight ... and I want to pick her up and run to safety ... but neither of us is capable of doing one thing to change this."

He enfolded me in his arms. "I'm sorry I can't fix this for us!"

"Honey, I couldn't fix it with my love, and unfortunately, neither can you."

I turned from his arms, and bent down to gently kiss Kim's forehead. Nothing soothed her pain. I stroked her arm, and listened while one agonizing groan after another emerged from her frail throat. When I couldn't bear to hear the sound of her travail any longer, I ran from the room, down the stairs, and out the Lobby door. I wanted the noise of the traffic whizzing by to drown out her echoing moans of pain, but her cries relentlessly drummed in my head. I surveyed the world around me, and once again found nowhere to run, and nowhere to escape the awful truth.

Within a few moments, Dan found me standing near the street. "Pam's taking care of Kim."

Taking my hand in his, he led me to the steps where we sat in silence outside the bustling hospital. Spring flowers were in bloom. Blades of newly mown grass waved in the breeze. Everything around me was sunny and bright while the light in my life was slowly being extinguished.

We watched lines of cars speed by. The traffic never stopped. Everywhere we turned, people were busily involved with their own lives. I shuddered at the absurdity. Our whole world was wrapped up in a tiny room on the second floor of this hospital, and yet, life on the outside remained the same. People worried about their bills, gardens, and taxes. Mothers shopped; couples enjoyed an evening out, and others went about their daily activities. How is it possible for life to keep marching on while our world is falling apart?

Dan squeezed my hand. "Babe, you're shaking! I've got a room at the hotel across the street. Let me take you there so you can get some rest, and I'll come back to stay with Kim."

I shook my head in protest, but he pulled me to my feet. "You need a break. Come on," he insisted. I had no choice but to follow.

The moment we stepped across the threshold of the room, something snapped inside of me. I screamed and cried; I could neither stop, nor hold back the pain exploding in my heart. Dan cradled me in his arms as I continued to scream while stifling the sound against his heaving chest.

I sobbed, "I cannot, and do not want to live without Kim!"

My words cut Dan to the core, yet he gently reminded me of our blessings. "We need you too, honey. You have two other kids to love, and take care of. You know … it can't be a coincidence that God gave us another little girl at the same time Kimmie got sick."

His words were a startling reminder of the same trite consolation friends and acquaintances offered on a daily basis. Did everyone truly believe the baby could somehow be a replacement for Kim? Each of our children was uniquely made and gifted by God. Each shared a special place in our lives.

Seething with anguish, the words from my internal conflict erupted. "There's room enough in my heart for *three* children! I have enough love for all three! You, Dirk, and Kim, have been my life; I can't give up part of that!"

Dan jerked me back into reality with his terse reply, "You have to; you have no choice!"

My fists pounded into his chest as I physically rejected the truth while my husband's arms engulfed me. His one lone tear trickled down my brow and mingled with the torrents gushing from me. Our bodies shuddered against one another in unspeakable anguish.

He was right. I had been fighting as though my holding on could make a difference. Kim had cancer, and no amount of wishing or hoping, could change that fact. I needed to accept it—not only in my mind—but also in my heart.

CHAPTER 32 - THE HOMEWARD JOURNEY

The moment I dreaded the most catapulted toward us. Dr. Carlton completed the arrangements for Kim's transfer within two days. On Wednesday, the eighth day of May, stark reality descended and pushed away the last vestige of my blind denial.

I vehemently fought against her transfer, first with one excuse and then another, but I understood the real reason behind my reluctance. If we took Kim home, I must face the ultimate truth: Nothing more could be done. We were in essence taking her home to die.

I considered this to be an act of surrender. Death poised itself to win, while I waved the white flag. A further truth loomed close at hand. I must return to face a world without Kim, and enter a home rendered less noisy, and more barren than I dared imagine.

Nurses filtered in and out of the room all morning to visit Kim and proffer their goodbyes. But when the moment of actual departure came, those closest to us were nowhere to be found. Two unfamiliar aides entered the room pushing a rolling bed. Both moved with proficiency to move Kim from her bed to the gurney. Dan held me while I quaked at her sharp groans. Why did no one understand she was in tremendous pain?

When the guard rails were snapped into their locked positions, Dan released me and ran down the stairs to bring the car around to the emergency entrance. The main hall of the pediatric wing appeared strangely vacant. I looked toward the nurses' station before entering the elevator; the desks and surrounding counter were devoid of all human activity. I understood. Their loss equaled ours. The final farewell would have been harrowing for each of us.

The drive home traumatized Kim. The car's continuous movement heightened the tortuous pain in her body. I cradled her in my arms in an attempt to shield her from the grueling torment. Dan slowed to a crawl for every bump and curve in the road, but nothing diminished the relentless agony she endured.

Following two hours of punishing travel, we reached the city limits, and veered northwest rather than driving to our ultimate destination. Dan and I needed to make one important stop before going to the hospital. We wanted Kim to meet the baby she had loved and prayed for every day.

After tenderly placing Kim on the back seat of the car, I solemnly walked into Mom and Dad's home. A few moments later, I emerged with the baby in my arms, and laid her beside Kim. The sisters lay face to face. Kristi kicked her feet against the seat and softly cooed. She was fascinated with her big sister. Her eyes never averted from Kim's face. A natural affinity drew the two sisters together.

"Kimmie, this is your baby sister, Kristi. She is smiling at you."

We never knew for certain whether Kim had any vision, and her pain was so tremendous at this point she might not have completely understood … but perhaps she felt the tiny hand that reached out and gently touched her face.

We drove the short distance to the hospital. Nurses were standing on alert at the emergency entrance for our arrival. They immediately transported Kim to a private room with a second bed for me.

Unable to function, I walked around in a daze. Overwrought from watching Kim's struggle, my senses shut down. Dan took charge; he oversaw every detail of the admission while he held me securely upright with one arm. The entire hospital staff moved in unison to assist us. They offered us coffee, juice and food; most importantly, they offered kindness and compassion.

Dr. Paul arrived shortly before noon. He was a familiar and comforting sight to a heartbroken mother. Stepping into the room, he gave my shoulder a reassuring squeeze before turning his attention to Kim. With her condition quite apparent, he completed his exam quickly.

Dr. Paul dangled Kim's medical file at his side, and tapped it against his left leg while he gave his assessment. "We are going to do everything possible to get you through this; we'll start by taking good care of Kim. First, we need to make her more comfortable. I'm ordering medication to take care of her pain immediately."

Dan and I breathed a sigh of relief. At last someone understood. Kim's pain had increased dramatically. Within fifteen minutes of Dr. Paul's directive, a nurse administered the medication, but it had little to no effect. Kim's prolonged groaning relentlessly echoed throughout the day. Agony racked her body.

At three o'clock in the afternoon, Dad brought Dirk to the hospital to visit his sister. Dan and I, along with Dad, stood at the room's entrance to give the two siblings' visit as much privacy as possible. For the first time in days, Kim's groans ceased. She listened with rapt attention to Dirk.

In his "big brother" voice, he bravely pronounced, "Hi, Kim, it's about time you got home." Pushing his thumbs in the front pockets of his jeans, he implored, "Hurry up and get well! I miss you."

I buried my face in Dan's chest to stifle the screeching cries threatening to erupt. I couldn't protect either child from this heartrending farewell.

Dirk's bravado melted away. He held Kim's hand for lingering moments while speaking private words to his little sister. His free hand tenderly stroked her arm. Had it been possible, I believe Dirk would have placed his arm over her shoulder while he said, "It's okay Kim; I'm bigger than you. You're gonna be okay; I'll take care of you."

He fell silent, then stood on tiptoes to lean closer to her. He gently laid his face cheek to cheek with hers. "I love you Kim," he whispered.

Dirk straightened from his embrace, and looked forlornly toward us. Neither Dan, nor I could muster words of comfort. Instead, we gathered our son into our arms. We feared this might be the last time he would be able to see his sister. This was not the way we wanted him to remember his beloved Kim.

Dad intervened, "Come on big boy; let's go see if Ben needs help at the store."

Dirk turned once more toward his sister before exiting the room. "See you later Kim."

CHAPTER 33 - HER HEART
YEARS FOR HOME

The sound of agonizing wails, along with turbulence in the pit of our stomachs, encompassed our days.

Kim's pain never withdrew nor subsided; we watched her abdomen enlarge daily. Dr. Paul increased the pain medication, but nothing dulled her agony.

Friends came by often; few stayed long. They found it too difficult to watch our little girl suffer such an ordeal. Indeed, by the end of the week the advanced stage of cancer was not a pleasant sight. Kim's tremors returned with increased intensity, and her limbs were drawn in rigidity.

This was a difficult time for each family member, and emotions were strained to the limit. I am positive we were unfair to many of the nurses when they struggled to care for Kimmie; nevertheless, they were true angels of mercy. Stalwart friends, whom God sent our way to assist and comfort us, were steadfast. Designated ones babysat Dirk and Kristi so my parents could visit, and others volunteered to stay with Kim while we rested or ate.

Dr. Paul exercised exceptional kindness. He understood not only the physical and mental strains encumbering us, but the financial one as well. He helped make each of our decisions easier. When I needed his advice, he simply pulled up a chair, sat down and answered my questions.

I remember with clarity one of the first things he said to us upon our arrival. "I know you two don't want Kim in a nursing home, so just forget about it. We'll take care of her here, or at home, for as long as necessary. If you want to take her home, I'll come to your house every day to check on her."

He pointed toward me. "You already know how to administer her feedings. I'll teach you how to give injections for her pain. If she needs any specialized care, we can find you a nurse. We *will* get you through this!"

Dr. Paul's calm assurances instantly removed a giant weight from us. God wrapped us in his love through the people he placed in our lives.

On Friday, with Dr. Paul's approval, We made the decision to take Kim home. The last three months had been my training period. I could manage her daily care as well as anyone.

We immediately mobilized our plans. One of our bedrooms needed to be equipped with a customized bed and suctioning apparatus, along with other necessary supplies. Volunteers rallied to help us by dividing the tasks among themselves. Some sat with Kim while we made the necessary preparations, and others helped with the cleaning and furniture arrangements. We thanked God for his many blessings.

I never left Kim for an extended time without preparing her for my departure. On Saturday morning, I explained my reason for leaving. "Honey, I have a surprise. Daddy and I are getting your room ready so we can take you home."

She determinedly moved her head up and down, signaling agreement.

"You and I are so tired of hospitals, and I just know you will get better as soon as you are home. There won't be any more strangers. Daddy and I will be with you all the time. Granny and Pawpaw can bring Dirk and the baby to see you more often too. Maybe Dirk can even spend the night with you. And of course, Missy can snuggle with you too."

Kim's head never stopped its upward and downward movement while I spoke.

"Sweetie, I haven't been able to rock you lately because it hurts you so much to be moved, but once we are home, things will be different. You will have a big bed in your room, and I will lie down beside you so we can cuddle and keep each other warm. We will read your favorite books, or listen to records. Would you like that?"

I watched her face flush. Her mouth drew downward in a familiar pout, and tears welled in her eyes. She was crying!

Her reaction offered all the encouragement I needed. Family and friends worried about our decision to care for Kim at home, but now that I understood how much it meant to her, I was willing to do it regardless of the hazards.

Within hours, volunteers transformed our master bedroom into a specialized care unit with a double bed for Kim, a twin bed for me, a chair, and all the necessary medical equipment. Only one finishing detail was missing. We ordered a pair of guard rails for her bed, but we weren't given a definite delivery date. Dr. Paul wouldn't allow us to take her home without this safeguard.

Over the weekend we made a point of reassuring Kim about our plans to take her home soon. Friends tried to dissuade us from the move, but aside from my fatigue, I had no real fears. I looked death squarely in the face, and knew it was sure to come. Our responsibility was to make it easier for Kim. We hoped the bed rails might be delivered on Monday so we could at long last bring our child home.

Monday arrived, but in the early morning hours, Kim's temperature spiked. Tests revealed an infection, so her transfer to our home was delayed. In spite of the medication being administered, her fever began to spiral out of control. By three o'clock in the afternoon, her temperature reached one hundred and five degrees; at six o'clock, her fever skyrocketed to one hundred and eight degrees.

Dr. Paul was summoned. "Let's get her packed in ice! We've got to get this temp down!"

Nurses lined both sides of Kim's body with ice packs, and her temperature began to steadily lower. When her fever dropped to a safer level, friends sat with Kim while Dan and I drove home for a quick meal and shower. Within thirty minutes, the hospital called.

"Kim's breathing is labored, and her pulse is rapid," a nurse informed us.

We sped to the hospital while I repeatedly begged, "Please, merciful Father, get us there in time. Don't let Kim die without her Daddy and me!"

With Dan clasping my hand and pulling me forward, we barreled breathlessly into the hospital room. Nurses and friends formed a circle around Kim's bed. They stepped aside to allow us closer access to her while we watched our child struggle for air.

Each breath came with a sharp gasp while she strained with her entire body to pull oxygen into her lungs. Each exhale brought the same horrifying groan as the pain enveloped her. I watched Kim struggle, witnessed the pain she suffered, and could not stop myself from begging God not to take her.

"No, Lord, not now! O dear God, I love her!"

My parents entered the circle to stand beside us. The room turned black; I drew in great gulps of air to stave off the panic.

Kimmie, I love you so very much! You are a part of my very soul. Why can't I curl up in the bed beside you and breathe for you?

Each delayed breath had me wondering if it was her last. Had the moment arrived when she would leave me forever?

Self-loathing gripped me. Why am I standing over my daughter like a vulture waiting for the angel of death to come and take her from me? She should not have to do this alone! I was sedated at Kim's birth when her first breath of life came rushing in. Now I watched as perhaps her last breath ebbed away… and just as before … I was totally helpless.

God answered my prayer. He did not take her on this particularly foreboding night. Within a few hours, her breathing stabilized, and our family and friends exited to allow us private time with our child.

We watched and waited. I stood beside Kim—holding my breath between each rise and fall of her chest. Dan sat in a chair with one leg folded across his other knee. His foot dangled in constant motion while his lips unconsciously whistled, "Sthhh, Sthhh."

"Father, help us," I silently prayed.

"You know," Dan drawled while motioning toward the other side of the room, "that extra bed over there is for you. You need to use it, and get some rest. I'll watch Kim."

"Honey, you've been here all day too. Why don't you go home for a few hours?"

"And leave you here by yourself? No!" He pointed once again toward the bed. His stare quashed any argument, so I reluctantly stretched out on the bed, and feigned rest.

Satisfied, he pushed his chair to the side of Kim's bed and sat watch over her while tenderly caressing her hand. He calibrated his breathing to match her's.

At midnight, I spoke from across the room. "Dan, you're

exhausted. Go home and lie down. Kimmie's holding her own for now."

"I'm staying here."

"You're about to fall out of that chair."

"I'm not really tired; I'm just sick of hospitals. I can't do diddly squat to help her. I'm as useless as a guard dog without a bark."

I smiled through the tears. "You're helping her the best way you can. Honey, go home, and get some rest. We'll be okay. I may need you more tomorrow."

Dan rose from the chair, bent down and planted a kiss on Kim's forehead, then gently squeezed her hand before pivoting his gaze toward me. "You call me if you need me. I can be here in five minutes. You don't have to do this alone."

"I know. I've never been alone. I don't know what I would do without you."

CHAPTER 34 - SWEETLY
CALLING FOR ME

My eyes focused solely on Kim. I watched her chest—waiting for every rise and fall—while listening to each wail of anguish. I stood hovering over her until my legs could hold me no longer.

Katie, the nurse on duty, took it upon herself to care for Kim exclusively through the night. She urged me to lie down. "Kim will need you more in the hours ahead. Get some rest while you can. I'll wake you if her condition changes."

Although I could not even think of sleep, I attempted to rest. Kim was in the compassionate and gentle care of a former high school classmate and friend. Katie turned Kim onto her right side. She now faced the windows instead of my bed. After making sure Kim was properly supported, the nurse quietly left the room.

Within seconds of Katie's departure, a sound emerged from across the room. "Mu ... Mu."

This was not Kim's customary moan, but rather, it sounded very much like a word. Over the previous ten weeks, Kim never managed more than a guttural "Un-uh," meaning "no". This sound was different.

I jumped up from the bed, and lunged toward Kim. It definitely sounded as though she was trying to call my name! I leaned closer to hear every syllable.

Kim persistently uttered the sound, "Mu … Mu …, Mu … Mu."

I stroked her hand. "Kimmie, I'm here."

The strange sound ceased. I reprimanded myself for having jumped to such a silly conclusion: You've yearned so long to hear Kim speak your name that you'll believe any new sound is the word you want to hear! I slipped quietly back into bed.

"Mu … Mu …, Mu … Mu."

I shot up from the bed. "Kimmie, I'm here honey. I love you."

This same sound emerged from Kim time after time throughout the following hour. Each time I stepped to her side and leaned over the bed, the sound ceased. When I briefly walked away to stretch the tightened muscles in my shoulders and legs, she repeated the same haunting cry, "Mu … Mu."

I dared to hope this was Kim's way of calling for me whenever she sensed I was not beside her. In my heart I believed she was summoning me. My prayers were being answered.

Triumph quickly turned to terror. My child was calling for me in answer to my stubborn petition before God throughout the long and difficult weeks of Kim's illness. My beautiful child at long last pleaded for me, but I could not console her—either by close proximity, touch, or word!

I needed to find a way to offer Kim comfort and to distract her from the pain. Nurses warned me, "Your weight on the bed could cause Kim greater agony." But I could not bear to hear her calling for me one moment longer.

Terrified of inflicting further pain upon my child, I held my breath, and gingerly lowered myself onto the bed beside Kim. I placed my arm gently on her back and drew her to me. I planted kiss upon kiss on her cheek and forehead while I held her.

"Mommy's here. I love you. It's all right Kim; go to sleep sweetie. I'll be right here beside you."

Kim's echoing cry ceased; her body relaxed.

"Kimmie, do you remember when we walked to the park on warm afternoons? You and Dirk jumped up on the merry-go-round, and I pushed and pulled on the heavy wheel to make it move. You laughed and said, 'Go round and round again Mom!' Honey, would you like to hear a song about going round and round? Hmm, let's see ..."

> *"Dirk and Kim on the Merry-GO-Round,*
> *Round and round, round and round.*
> *Swinging and sliding, and racing around,*
> *Won't it be fun going round and round?'*

> *"Rocking your sister, and feeding her too,*
> *Hand in hand, just Kristi and you.*
> *Kisses and hugs all the day through,*
> *Going round and round singing I love you.*

> *"Daddy will twirl you round and round,*
> *Throw you high, and catch you sound.*
> *Hug you, kiss you, and set you down.*
> *Won't it be fun going round and round?"*

Chapter 35 - Tic-Tic-Whoosh

The morning sun peeped through the windows, but its brilliance could not penetrate the sorrow in our lives. Dan arrived shortly before seven. He anxiously paced the distance from Kim's bed to the doorway. Looking at our child, we easily ascertained something other than the brain tumor afflicted her. Kim's abdominal circumference grew by the hour. The largest diaper available could no longer close around her waist.

Dr. Paul entered our room on his morning rounds at nine o'clock. After examining Kim, he gave a directive to the attending nurse. "We need to get a stomach pump in here stat."

Dan clinched my hand in his strong grip. "What's wrong?"

Dr. Paul folded his arms across his chest. "You won't need the room at home after all. Her colon is completely blocked by an obstruction. This most likely means the cancer has metastasized. You won't have to wait much longer."

Unable to speak, Dan and I silently stared into space.

Suddenly, with every ounce of the same bitterness I felt brewing in my own heart, Dan spewed, "I don't see why God doesn't just take her if it's what He wants! Why does she have to suffer?"

This was decidedly a bitter pill to swallow. The agony Kim endured thus far was bad enough, but now she experienced excruciating pain. We watched as the nurses performed humiliating, mandatory procedures while remembering the brave, determined little girl who once ran into our arms. Kim must hate all the probing and poking, and yet she could do nothing about it. She could neither ask them to stop, nor move her hands in protest.

Several nurses admitted, "Before we were assigned to your daughter, we frequently wondered what the others became so excited about. We never saw any real change in her just from passing glances, but the more we observed Kim, the more we became aware of her willful spirit clinging to life."

Even now as she lay so near death, her spirit lived on.

As it became more evident her pain had reached intolerable heights, I asked a nurse to give Kim more medication. Within moments, the charge nurse appeared to personally answer my request.

"Mr. and Mrs. Grissom, I know it looks as though Kim is in extreme discomfort, but because of the high temperatures she's experienced, it's highly unlikely she is able to feel any pain. At this point your daughter can't possibly be aware of her surroundings."

Even so, as the nurse lingered, her eyes repeatedly darted toward the bed on which Kim lay. Before long, she stepped over to the bed, observed her momentarily, and instructed a second nurse to administer more medication immediately.

Throughout the day, the room echoed with the sounds of Kim's tormented groans, and the soft "Tic-tic-whoosh" of the stomach pump. Her suffering rent my heart asunder; a sickening bitterness floated in the pit of my stomach. My soul longed for rest from all the heartache. My chest ached with unshed tears. Oh, if I could just carry her away to safety! But Kimmie had no avenue of escape, and I must stop being the coward. Time staggered by, one "Uhhhh" and one "Tic-tic-whoosh" at a time.

Dan stood vigilantly beside us. The constant sound of the machine's pumping frazzled our nerves. Tensions mounted. At four in the afternoon, he vaulted from his chair, lunged toward the window, and through gnashed teeth growled, **"Dear God, why does Kimmie have to suffer? Hasn't she been through enough?"**

Words failed me. Dan echoed my exact thoughts. I sailed toward him and simply leaned my head on his shoulder.

He wrapped his arm around me and murmured, "If there was somebody doing this to her, I could take a baseball bat and knock him into next Sunday. But there's not anyone, and that makes me as worthless as a peach orchard borer."

Oh Lord, save us from our wretchedness. We are helpless. Help us! We are weak. Be our strength. We are hopeless. Instill us with faith.

"Dan, you're not worthless. Kim adores you, and she knows you're here. That's what matters. But, you've paced across this room, and up and down the hall a million times. Honey, go somewhere. Drive around town. Mow the lawn, or go check on the kids. Just get away from here for a little while. This place will drive you crazy."

Reluctantly, he followed my suggestion. "I guess I need to go by and see the kids, then check the shop to make sure no one's needed anything today."

I sat alone with Kim when the doctor made his evening rounds. Thinking we might not be able to absorb everything at once, Dr. Paul withheld a portion of his assessment earlier in the day. On this visit, he informed me it was no longer possible to feed Kim through the nasogastric tube.

"The cancer's completely blocked the colon. If we continue feeding her, the food has no place to go. This child has suffered enough. I can't recommend giving her intravenous fluids either. It will only prolong her suffering and death. It's better for all concerned if this is over as quickly as possible."

The remaining snippet of reasoning ability I possessed took over. I calmly nodded my head in agreement. Yes, it was the right thing—the only thing to do. Kim had suffered long enough. Dan and I could not bear to see her in such pain.

Wisdom demanded Dr. Paul's approach become the only choice, yet my heart screamed otherwise when I sought to explain the situation to others. Reason gave way to a terrible, crushing truth: After all the endless days of tests, pain, surgeries, and suffering, Kim must meet death through starvation.

I couldn't sugar-coat it; she would starve to death. For months I had been clinging to my faith, and holding on to the knowledge that God does not place more on us than we can bear. Now, however, I knew I had reached my limit; I could go no further. I could not stand the thought of Kimmie dying without food or water.

"No, Lord, no," I cried. "You can't let this happen!"

My hopes were shattered. Kim was destined to walk through the dark shadow of death, a pathway on which we could not accompany her, but she would not travel alone. Jesus stood ready to walk with her, and encompass her with his presence. I was ready at last to give her to Jesus … fully and completely … without reservation.

CHAPTER 36 - THE HEART SHATTERS

Friends, Beverly and Joyce, dropped by to give me respite. Beverly proffered a hug, along with a knowing smile. "We're here so you can go home to eat a bite, and then rest a little while."

I welcomed their loving gesture. My heart was racing, and about to explode. I needed a place of privacy where I could weep until I extinguished the burning anguish in my heart.

I don't remember the drive home. I couldn't concentrate on anything other than the death awaiting Kimmie. I only remember the searing urgency to reach the door of our home. I blindly propelled myself over the threshold, and closed the door behind me. My heart was too shattered to utter a sound. I dropped to the floor, raised my head and hands toward heaven, and silently pleaded with my Savior.

> *"Lord, you know better than anyone the trauma awaiting Kim. When you were on the cross, you said, '...I thirst' (John 19:28 KJV). Lord, Kim is thirsty. Please Jesus, give her something to drink! Rescue her. Don't let her suffer anymore! Sweep her into your arms, and hide her in your sheltering wings."*

Tears flowed freely while my throat constricted with a stifled scream, but I had no time to waste. I must return to Kimmie as quickly as possible. I pulled myself up from the floor, and walked toward our bedroom. After a quick shower and a change of clothes, I wandered mindlessly into the kitchen. I needed to warm something for Dan to eat. Church members kept us abundantly supplied with salads and casseroles.

Dan opened the front door, and treaded toward the kitchen. He took one look at me, and worriedly inquired, "Babe, what's wrong? What's happened?"

"Dr. Park came by to see Kim again this afternoon."

"What's wrong? What did he say?"

"Kimmie's going to starve to death! He said her colon is too blocked to feed her. The food has nowhere to go. He doesn't want to feed her intravenously either. He said it would only prolong her suffering."

Dan's expletive reverberated throughout the kitchen. I bit my lower lip, and blinked back tears.

He pressed his hand over his face and muttered, "Nobody deserves to suffer like she has! I just want it to end. I've never felt so helpless in my life."

He strode toward me, clasped me by the shoulders and declared, "You just remember one thing. We weren't going to put her in a nursing home, and we have the final say on this too. Kimmie's our baby!"

I leaned my head on his shoulder for comfort. Tears spilled down my cheek as I answered with a trembling voice, "I know honey. Dr. Paul's just doing what he thinks is best. He's only putting on his shoulders something we could never be brave enough to do. Cancer is the real culprit here."

"I told you from the beginning that there's nothing good in any of this."

"I know Dan, but I keep hearing Kim's plea in the hospital before her first surgery. It never stops ringing in my ears. *'Mommy! Mommy! I'm thirsty!'* I don't want her to die like this!"

"What do you want me to do? I'll talk to Dr. Paul."

"There's nothing we *can* do now. We can't do anything until the stomach pump is removed."

"I don't think there's an easy way to die with cancer, and I guess Dr. Park is right ... but I wish God would just take her out of this misery!"

"Maybe that's what we need to do—pray and ask God to take her home so she won't have to suffer anymore."

We held each other as we bowed our heads to pray, but our words faltered. How could we ask such a thing? Dan at last spoke. "Dear God, we don't know what to ask. We just don't want her to suffer anymore. We need your help."

Disinclined to eat, we sat staring at the food on the table. Dan murmured, "We have another problem."

"What?"

"Dirk."

My head jerked upward in full alert. "What's wrong?"

"He doesn't talk much anymore; he keeps to himself. He knows last night was bad for Kim."

I shuddered while tears dripped from my eyes. Will this nightmare not end until it destroys us all?

"Honey, we have to help him! In a lot of ways, this has been harder on Dirk than on us. He came home from school one day, and Kim was gone. She's never going to come home again."

Dan nodded, "I'll go by and check on him and Kristi again before I come to the hospital. I'm staying with you and Kim tonight. I need to tell your folks what's going on with Kim anyway."

"Lord, help me. I'm torn between my children, and I don't

know which one needs me more!" I placed my hand on his. "Do you know the best way you could help me tonight? Take care of Dirk. Let him have a few hours of normalcy—if there is such a thing anymore."

He exhaled a faltering breath. "And I need to be in two places at once too, but you're right. He needs to get away for a while. Your Mom's phone never stops ringing, and people are coming in and out all day long. He hears everything that's said.

"I want to see Kim again, and then I'll bring him home with me. We'll play ball, or something else. But, I think he needs to sleep at your folk's house tonight—just in case you need me."

"I'll always need you, but right now Dirk needs you more. Kristi is too young to understand, but how can a six-year-old cope when his world has collapsed? We made a pact in the beginning to take care of *all* our kids. One of us should be with him tonight."

"Well," Dan paused in thought, "you're a lot better with hospitals than I am. Dirk's my boy. I think I need him more tonight than he needs me."

Father, the storm is rising—billowing and frothing around us. It threatens to drown us in its wake. Part the seas so we might walk safely through the deep waters.

Let us push forward toward your loving hand. Help us safely cross onto dry ground. Shelter us from the storm.

Drown our enemies of fear and destruction. Be thou our mighty Lord and Savior, for we are helpless.

Why O Lord, do we toil and struggle? Why do we not rest in your arms?

O Lord, save us from ourselves. Rescue us from the depths of despair! Show thy face; extend thy hand of mercy. Open the portals of heaven and let us glimpse your glory!

CHAPTER 37 - NOTHING IS TOO HARD FOR GOD

In less than one hour, I drove back to the hospital and entered Kim's room. Friends were seated beside her bed, and I greeted them first before turning toward Kim. I found it impossible to look at her now without giving way to tears. I took a deep breath to steady my quivering voice, then touched my daughter's hand. "Kimmie, I'm here. I told you I would be back very soon. Daddy will be here in a little while to see you. I love you honey."

One very dear man among the friends assembled around Kim caught my attention. Brother Cliff and his wife Beverly had visited, and stood with us through many storms. This compassionate deacon enjoyed a profound relationship with Jesus Christ. Intuitively, I understood his being in the room was no accident. God provided the perfect person to pray the words we could not bear to speak.

Dan and I attempted to pray at dinner, but the words stuck in our throats. Neither of us were able to expel the words, "Take her!" We needed someone outside the family—someone who could not feel the pain as intensely as we did—to help guide this prayer.

When he stood to greet me, I asked, "Would you mind walking with me to the chapel while Beverly stays with Kim?"

Without hesitation, he replied, "That's why I'm here."

We did not leave the room immediately. First, God granted me the one request I had so often laid before his throne. I leaned over the bed to explain my reason for leaving again so quickly.

"Honey, I will be back in just a few minutes. Cliff and I are going down to the chapel to talk to Jesus about you."

Kim instantly rolled her eyes toward me and began moving her head slowly back and forth signaling *"No"* while uttering the sound, "Un-uh."

I reached down to console my sweet child. Hugging her close to me, I spoke softly. "It's okay sweetie; Mommy just wants to talk to Jesus about getting you well. I will be back very soon, and I promise I won't leave again."

The more I tried to console Kim, the more agitated she became. In the midst of her distress came the words, "Un-uh Mom! Un-uh Mom!"

I dared not believe. I looked into the faces of the others gathered around the room. Their astonished looks and smiles confirmed I had not imagined it. Kim called my name, and pleaded with me not to leave her!

Brother Cliff vocally sounded everyone's amazement. "That little girl understands you, and she doesn't want you to leave!"

Except for the groans of travail, and a rare "Un-uh," our loving child had not spoken a word in almost three months. We were told it was both medically and physically impossible for her to speak. Yet defying all odds and medical diagnosis, Kimmie spoke!

It was absolutely and utterly impossible! It could not be done! Yet, "… with God all things are possible" (Mark 10:27). He is "… able to do exceeding abundantly above all that we ask or think …" (Eph. 3:20).

Rivulets of tears streamed from every eye in the room.

God's marvelous love reached down from above. His hand touched our daughter's lips, and she spoke!

Kim did not actually speak the words I requested. She did not say the words, "I love you," but you can't out give God. He permitted Kim to speak while expressing her love in a much better way. I heard my child call my name!

"Mom" is the sweetest sound on earth when a child speaks it in love.

"Oh Kimmie, my precious baby, I heard you honey! I have waited so long to hear your voice again! Sweetie, I love you! I love you so very much!"

I kissed her in rapt joy again and again while praising God with each breath. How can you give enough praises to the loving and magnificent God who makes all things possible?

Kim's speaking created a great dilemma. Do I stay in this room or obey the urging of the Holy Spirit? She pleaded with me not to abandon her, yet my heart weighed heavy. Jesus was summoning me to prayer, but after hearing Kimmie's voice, nothing could pry me from her side.

I wiped away tears of joy, and looked once more toward my precious child. Her beautiful face was strangely veiled. I saw nothing other than the ravages of end stage cancer—her pitifully swollen tummy, her hands clenched into fists, and her precious body enduring ceaseless tremors. The veil lifted to reveal Kim's dry and cracked lips. I heard the anguished struggle with each breath she took. If my Savior did not intervene, Kim might linger in indescribable suffering. My heart was torn asunder by an internal struggle requiring more fortitude than I possessed.

"Oh God, please help Kimmie understand and forgive me

for leaving her again! I don't want to walk away from her and turn my back upon her plea, but I can't let her continue to suffer such agony! Please Lord Jesus, hold her hand while I do the impossible."

My love for Kim demanded I act in her best interest. I must leave my precious child long enough to bare my heart before God. At dinner, Dan and I made the decision to pray for her release from torment. As much as I wanted to hold on to her forever, my love for her could no longer be selfishly wrapped up in my needs. The ultimate way to love Kim ... to tenderly care for her ... was to release my hold upon her, and place her in the hands of Jesus.

Aware of my struggle, Cliff walked over to the bed, and gently touched my shoulder. "I'm in no hurry. You stay with her as long as you need to. I'll go get a cup of coffee."

I tearfully offered a smile in appreciation of his kindness.

I took Kimmie's hands in mine to gently sooth her fears while savoring this moment and locking it tightly in my heart. "Kimmie, Mom will never go far away from you; I love you too much. Remember, you are my precious little helper. We always do things together, and that is why I need to walk down the hall for just a minute. I need to ask God to make you feel better so you can run and play again. It hurts my heart to see you so sick."

Listening to every word, Kim inclined her head toward me. I paused briefly to kiss her cheek, and give her a gentle hug.

"Kimmie, I love you with a forever love. I will only be a few steps away, and I am leaving Jesus here to hold your hand while I am gone. He loves you so very much, and I know he will take good care of you.

"I promise I will be back in just a few minutes. Mom, Daddy, and Dirk want you to feel better. Your head and tummy have hurt long enough. We are very sad because you can't do the things you want to do.

"Do you remember what you learned in Bible School? You said it every morning when we washed the dishes. *'God made the flowers and trees, and He made me.'* God can make you feel better too."

Kim's agitation ceased. Her body began to relax beneath the touch of my hand.

"Father, I am so grateful to you for the opportunity to spend these last months with Kim. Her impassioned plea confirmed she unequivocally needed a mother—and not just any mother— *her mother!* How much better can anyone say, 'I love you'?'"

I tenderly touched, kissed, and hugged my sweet child until she was no longer afraid, but the "Un-uh" resumed when I stepped out of the room. I willed myself to turn my back against her plea. I must do this for my Kimmie! Friends, who sat with Kim while we were gone, said her eyes never wavered from the door until my return.

On the way to the chapel, I spoke with Cliff about the doctor's prognosis. When we neared the entrance, I turned to address the deacon directly. "With every trial we've gone through, I've cried out, 'Lord, I can't bear it!' Yet each time, God has shown me I could do even the impossible with his help.

"But now, I have nothing left. This time I know for certain the one thing ... the only thing ... I cannot bear, is to watch my child starve to death. Please pray with me that Kim will not have to die like this. I want her to leave us in love and with peace."

The dimly lit prayer room, with a single light burning in one corner, was my last refuge of hope. We knelt before a row of upholstered chairs; I bowed my head to pray, but the sorrow was too great for utterance. "Oh Lord!" I cried, before the tears streamed from a broken and battered heart.

Instantly, Christ's Spirit entered the room. Though our eyes were closed in prayer, we each saw a glow of brilliant light illuminate the chapel; this same light infused us with a comforting warmth.

Cliff began to pray. Many will find this difficult to believe, but I am certain the next occurrence was not of human kindness, but rather of divine guidance. Others can sympathize, but no one can fully comprehend the inexpressible sorrow in another person's heart. No one other than Jesus could have actually known my innermost thoughts.

As he prayed, every bit of anguish I felt came pouring from his soul. He begged; he pleaded with God to have mercy upon Kim. My heart became lighter with each word he spoke.

Abruptly, Cliff switched the direction of his prayer in midstream. One moment his prayer beseeched Christ on my behalf, then without pause, he began to deliver a message to me—directly from my Father:

> *"And they brought young children to him, that he should touch them: and his disciples rebuked those that brought them. But when Jesus saw it, he was much displeased, and said unto them, suffer the little children to come unto me, and forbid them not: for of such is the kingdom of God" (Mark 10: 13–14).*

Something touched my shoulder, and sent tremors throughout my body as he recounted the story of King David. "When David learned of his son's illness, he was distraught. Refusing to eat, he lay in supplication before God. But when David heard his child was dead, he stood up, dressed himself in clean clothes, and praised God" (2 Sam. 12:16, 18—20).

Quoting David's beloved words of comfort, the deacon delivered God's promise of reunion: "But now he is dead, wherefore should I fast? Can I bring him back again? I shall go to him, but he shall not return to me" (2 Sam. 12:23).

It gave me great comfort to know with certainty I could go to Kim one day. This separation was not permanent. One day I will join her in glory. Scripture upon scripture tumbled from Cliff's lips, reassuring my heart it was okay to let go. Our loving heavenly Father held Kim in his righteous right hand.

At last, I found the courage to close the prayer. "Father, you answered my plea to hear Kimmie speak once more. Now I know your angels are hovering close by. Soon my arms will no longer be able to hold our little girl. Cradle her in yours. Have your will Lord."

Cliff and I spoke briefly on our way back to the room. He could not remember most of the things he spoke in prayer, and in fact, he was dumbfounded by many of the words I repeated to him. But we were both certain of two things: Christ had entered the chapel, and we felt his presence.

Dan sat waiting in the room when we returned from the chapel. While Cliff relayed our experience, I sat down in a chair beside Kim, and took her hand in mine.

"Kimmie, Mommy's back—just like I promised. I didn't want to be away from you any longer. We talked to God about you, and he just told me you are going to feel better very soon. Don't worry honey; I'm not leaving again. I'm staying right here with you all night. I love you."

Kim's body relaxed. Her eyes closed in rest.

Peace engulfed me once more. This sustaining peace went beyond mortal comprehension. Those same words, "Everything is all right," were once again instilled in my heart. From the very beginning, I believed these words meant Kim would be healed.

Now I understood the full extent of their meaning. Everything was all right—not because she would be miraculously healed—but rather, because all things were unalterably in God's hands. No matter what tragedy struck … even if it was death … I could say, "Everything is all right." God was in control; I had no need to fear.

After watching Kim endure such agony, death no longer seemed ominous to me. I waited for her death—an end to all her suffering and pain. I understood her death meant only the freeing of her soul to be with her loving Father. If I loved Kim, how much more so must God love her? Yes, she was in good hands; I knew everything was all right.

Brother Cliff visited a few moments longer and offered a final prayer before his departure. Dan and I stood on opposite sides of the room staring at the walls. If our eyes ever met, the facades of bravery we wore might disintegrate. A dark shadow of approaching death hovered over us.

"Uh-hmm." Dan coughed to gain my attention, then motioned with his head toward the door. I followed him into the hallway. He spoke in a hushed tone to prevent Kim from hearing our conversation. "I'm staying with you tonight. I'll sit up with her so you can get some rest."

"We talked about this at supper. Dirk needs you tonight. He's always had a sixth sense about this. After last night's episode with Kim's breathing, he must be counting down the minutes too."

"I know. I'm just worried about you and Kim being all alone tonight."

"There are nurses everywhere, and I know if I call you, you'll be here before I can hang up the phone."

He nodded. "I just wanted to see my baby girl again, and tell her bye."

234

Acknowledging his need to be near Kimmie, I smiled through the tears.

His eyes stared piercingly into mine. "Are you sure you'll be okay by yourself?"

I leaned my head on his chest in reply.

His arms tightened around me. "Dear God," he whispered. "I wish we could take her home! Call me if you need me. I love you."

Stifling my tears, I replied, "I love you too. Give Dirk a big hug for me. Tell him I love him."

Dan shook his head. "I don't think he'll ever pick up his guitar again and play it without Kimmie there to dance."

He turned from the hall, stepped back into the room, and bent down to kiss Kim's cheek. "Night-night Sugar. Daddy loves you."

His voice crackled, "You'll always be Daddy's little girl. I'll see you in a little while."

My husband's feet were cemented to the floor. Sadness permeated the air. I locked my arms around his waist while we captured the image of our daughter, and pasted it into the albums of our souls.

"Babe, are you sure you want me to leave?"

"No honey; I'm not sure of anything, but right now, Dirk needs you more."

He tenderly held Kim's hand one last time before solemnly exiting the room, and I stood vigil with my precious daughter for one more night.

CHAPTER 38 - AT LAST I UNDERSTAND

Rest never entered my mind. I saw God's plan more clearly now than ever before. I planted myself beside Kim knowing there were mere hours remaining for me to share this earthly life with her. I could think of nothing new to say, only the same trite words spoken so many times before.

"I love you Kimmie Dawn. You are my precious little girl. I love you with all my heart. You make me smile; your sweet kisses and hugs make my heart sing.

"You will always be Daddy's little girl, and you are Mom's big helper. I just can't do anything without you."

"And you know what, Kim?"

"You love me. And you love Daddy. And you love Dirkie. And you love baby Kristi. And you love Granny and Pawpaw. And you love Grandma and Grandpa. And you love Missy.

"And you know what, Kim?"

"I love you. And Daddy loves you. And Dirkie loves you. And the baby loves you. And Granny and Pawpaw love you. And Grandma and Grandpa love you. And Missy loves you.

"And Kimmie, Jesus loves you too. He will make you well soon."

Kim's last night on earth was quiet. Only her soft moans from the interminable pain, and the "Tic-tic-whoosh" of the stomach pump interrupted the stillness. In the darkened hours, the Holy Spirit revealed certain things I had never contemplated before.

Looking into the eyes of my daughter, I witnessed the reflection of Christ. From an early age, my parents taught these two things: The goal is to become more like Christ. Follow his example.

Never before had I fully understood these commands nor applied them to my own life, but while I sat gazing upon my brave and dauntless child, God's Spirit filled my being. He pulled the layers of pain from my heart, and opened my spirit to the revealing truth in his Word.

Through anguished eyes, I focused solely upon Kim. Remorse filled my soul. I had lived upon this earth twenty-eight years, but it took a three-year-old child to show me how to behave like a Christian.

Until three days earlier, I was not aware Kimmie possessed the ability to cry. Through all the weeks of pain, suffering, and torment, not one tear trickled down her cheek. My sweet child never cried for herself. Her tears were shed for the first time at the mention of going home to be reunited with her family.

My heart thudded against my chest. I was the whiner and the complainer. I was the one who had daily pity parties … not my daughter. As Kim suffered through her greatest pinnacle of pain, she never once shed tears for herself; her tears were spilled only out of love for others.

Sadness spread over me when I thought of Christ dying on the cross and shedding tears—not for himself—but for each of us. This is our example of supreme love.

As he promised, Dan came back to the hospital after

spending the evening with Dirk. He held Kim's hand while unwittingly rubbing his thumb across her skin.

"Sugar, Daddy sure loves you. You're my little girl, and you always will be. I wouldn't trade you for anything. Dirk said to tell you he loves you. He misses you."

Convinced Kim was stable, he left at a quarter to midnight with one stipulation. "I want you to lie down. If you won't go home, you at least need to rest."

Shortly following his exit, a sound emerged above the noise of the stomach pump. "Uhhhh … Uhhhh," Kimmie groaned from across the room.

I slipped from the bed. "I'm here Kimmie. I'm not leaving you honey. I love you."

After midnight, when all was quiet in the halls, I lowered the guard rail, scooted a tall stool to the edge of Kim's bed, and sat down while leaning forward and contorting my upper body onto the bed so I could be as close to her as possible. I yearned to lie beside Kimmie one last time, but her pain, along with her ever increasing girth made it impossible. I could not willingly bring myself to add to her agony.

She softly murmured, "Mu … Mu."

I ran my fingers across her cheek and down her arm while she lay on her side facing me.

"Kimmie, at last I understand everything you were trying to tell me when you looked into my eyes after every kiss. Your eyes were the window through which I was given a tiny glimpse of God's unfathomable love. You came to show me what true love is. It's about loving others more than ourselves. Love always points toward Jesus.

"You are his perfect gift, sent down from heaven to bless our lives, and draw us closer to God. You are his emissary of love. I will never forget to tell everyone how God's love has surrounded us and held us together. And Kimmie, I will never, ever, forget the love you gave to me, Daddy, Dirkie, and the baby."

I choked back a threatening sob before whispering my impassioned words of goodbye: "Kimmie Dawn, I love you so much. You are my darling little girl. Do you remember Mom and Daddy's favorite picture of you? We were at Grandma and Grandpa's house on Christmas Eve. You were just a tiny little girl, not quite two years old. Daddy took a picture of you wearing a blue flannel nightgown, with a holster and two guns strapped around your waist, while you cuddled your favorite doll. That's our Kimmie, all sweetness with a little bit of spice— loving on your baby while you fought the bad guys with your brother.

"Sweetie, it won't be long until you are much better. You will run and play, and never be sick again. You will get to kiss Jesus and give him a hug.

"Kimmie, blink once, and I will be beside you. I will be there holding your hand as we walk to God's garden together. We will stop along the way and pick the pretty flowers, and pet every puppy and kitty you see. You will stand on my feet, and we will dance and sing. We will hug, kiss, and never get tired of saying, 'I love you.'

"Before you can blink again, Daddy will be there to tickle your feet, and squeeze you too *ruts*, because we know Daddy likes to play rough. He will carry you on his shoulders and play horsey until you squeal, 'Daddy, put me down!'

"Count to five honey, and Dirkie will be with you too. The two of you will run across the green grass and race to the gold sidewalk. This time Kimmie, because you are so strong, you will cross the finish line first, and your brother will be the first to congratulate you. When you count to five again, baby

Kristi will be there beside you. The two of you will stay up late giggling and sharing secrets, just like all sisters do.

"What a wonderful time we will have Kimmie, when Jesus makes you well, and he brings us all together again as a family. We will all live together as happy as we can be."

I inwardly sighed, gathering the strength to sing one more tuneless lullaby made up of words from the heartstrings of my soul.

> "Go to sleep my precious little girl; Mommy is here to watch over you. I love you; I love you Kimmie. Kimmie Dawn my sweet, sweet baby. Daddy, Mommy, Dirkie, and the baby will love you forever and ever. Go to sleep my precious little one. Jesus will take care of you."

The clock struck three in the morning. Darkness prevailed; it soaked my soul in gloom, and paralyzed me with dread. Following the nurse's visit, I lowered myself once more onto the bed. "Father, thank you for giving us this loving child."

My heart was so heavy I couldn't think of another word to say. Old hymns I played on the piano, and sang in my youth bubbled up from my soul—songs about love, trust, grace, and God's greatness.

While I lay beside my child softly humming one last song, I felt a sudden change in Kim. Sensing she had slipped silently away from me, I drew her nearer to my heart.

"Kimmie! Kimmie Dawn!" Silence answered back.

My palm fell on her chest. *She's still breathing!*

"Baby, are you with me? Mommy's here! Kimmie, I'm here baby!"

The room stood eerily still.

My heart perceived Kim no longer inhabited this world. She

stood waiting just outside heaven's door, and only her ravaged body constrained her from entering its gates. I rocked her back and forth in my arms.

"Oh Kimmie, I love you sweet baby! I love you! I will always love you!"

I gently and lovingly bathed her in the early morning of the new dawn. Since our arrival, the nurses insisted upon bathing Kim, but on this final morning they acquiesced. Understanding my need to bestow upon her whatever last touches of love I could give, the nurse in attendance simply stood back and observed.

As the linens were changed, I held Kimmie Dawn for the last time. I no longer sensed the presence of her spirit. The essence which once made her so unique had fled to a faraway place where my hands could not reach. Still, I caressed her tender body born of mine.

I trembled while pleading, "Help me Lord; hold back the tears. Give me the courage to be as strong as Kim."

Taking a deep breath, I searched for final words while bringing her hand to my lips for a kiss. "Sweetie, I'm not sure you can hear me now. Jesus helped you fall asleep. I am glad because you have hurt long enough.

"The next time you open your eyes, you will be well. You will wake up in a beautiful palace with golden stairs. Most importantly, you'll never need to be in a bed, or a hospital, again.

"You will find a big table full of all your favorite foods, and you will be able to eat anything you want. At the end of the table, a big bowl of green sherbet will be waiting for you. And I know God's table has lots of chocolate candy!

"You have fun running and playing. Twirl around and round in the beautiful park, and help Jesus take care of all the puppies. Remember honey, wherever you go, I will come and find you. I will hear your voice, and know you're my Kimmie. Nothing can ever separate us. One day I will hold you in my arms again. I will see you soon.

"Daddy, Dirkie, Kristi, Granny, Pawpaw, Grandma, Grandpa, and Missy love you. And Kimmie, you know Mommy will always and forever love you."

> *"And if I go and prepare a place for you, I will come again, and receive you unto myself; that where I am, there ye may be also" (John 14:3).*

CHAPTER 39 - ASK FOR ANYTHING

Dan arrived at the hospital shortly before eight in the morning. "I just stopped by your folk's house to check on the kids. They're fine. I'm staying with Kim this morning. I want you to go home and get some rest."

I was emotionally drained, but I could not leave. "Honey, I want to be here when the doctor comes by this morning. I need to know about Kim's condition."

Biting his lower lip, he nodded in agreement.

Within forty-five minutes, Dr. Paul appeared on his morning rounds. Miraculously, during his examination, the doctor discovered the blockage had decreased, and her colon was no longer completely obstructed.

He offered a tentative smile before stating, "I'm going to have the stomach pump removed, and order the hourly feedings to be resumed immediately."

Dan squeezed my hand in his firm grip. Relief flooded our souls. I stood in awe. WE SIMPLY ASKED, AND WE RECEIVED! "...: ask, and ye shall receive, that your joy may be full" (John 16:24).

I said a quick and silent "Thank you, Lord!" My mind could not comprehend the majesty of his great power. Our child was spared the grueling process of dying without fluids! God, in his mercy, answered our prayer.

I leaned over her bed. "Did you hear what the doctor said Kimmie? Jesus has made you better. They are bringing you water. Mom's going home for a little bit. I'll be back soon. Love you honey."

Intending to be gone only long enough for a shower and a quick change of clothes, I snatched my purse from the closet. In spite of Dan's insistence, I was determined to spend every possible moment with Kim. Her time could only be measured in hours.

With rapid force, the room began to whirl around me. Weariness overtook my body. No matter how I struggled, I found it impossible to put one foot in front of the other. Whether from physical exhaustion or the constant emotional stress, my body simply could not move.

When I began to sway, Dan gathered me in his arms. My legs turned to rubber. Both knees buckled, making it impossible for me to stand. Struggling to keep me erect, Dan tightened his arms around me as I stumbled beside him. When I continued to falter, he ultimately lifted me in his arms, and carried me through the corridor and to the car.

I leaned my head against the passenger's window in an attempt to steady my reeling brain while Dan lectured me all the way home.

"I want you to stay in bed and get some rest! This isn't going to get any easier. You're going to need your strength later to get through this. I know you. I know you haven't slept at all in the last forty-eight hours. More than likely, it's been at least a week since you've even tried to sleep. You never eat anything either; you're as skinny as a rail! Dirk is going to need you, and I need you too!"

His anger was not directed toward me. Everything had spiraled out of his control, and now his world, along with mine, lay in a crumbled heap. The instant he had me safely tucked in bed with instructions to "stay put," he spun around on his heels to speed back to the hospital.

Why must I be cursed with this weak body? I've been at the hospital twenty-four hours a day for months, alone, without respite, and now at this crucial time, my body chooses to betray me! Tears of frustration and grief poured from me, but in the end, I was too exhausted to move. My will to fight evaporated.

Although the darkness of oblivion circled, I needed to thank God for his mercy. Lacking the strength to audibly express my appreciation; my spirit silently spoke my gratitude.

"Thank you Father, for understanding my silent groans last night. Thank you for not allowing our child to starve to death. Lord, I can hardly take it all in. Thanks to you, Kim is receiving fluids into her parched and dehydrated system. Thank you for not allowing her to endure any further suffering! I don't think she feels any pain now. Thank you for your unending love!"

Part of my brain understood the removal of fluids while Kim was on the stomach pump hastened her present condition; nevertheless, I knew God played a greater part in this situation.

Darkness engulfed me. My body trembled and shook; the room whirled in a dizzying blur, but rest eluded me. I could not separate the fatigue from my guilt over leaving Kim.

The rushing current grabbed hold, pulling me under, and like a drowning victim, I became too powerless to fight the undertow. Eventually, I gave in to the inevitable and allowed myself to drift into nothingness.

In the blurred place of emotional and physical exhaustion, one never finds rest. The body shuts down; the eyes may close, but the mind churns over things it cannot change, and the heart never stops yearning.

Two interruptions dragged me from my languor. Dan came

home around eleven o'clock for an early lunch. Forbidding me to get out of bed, he hastily took a slice of ham from the refrigerator and stuffed it between two pieces of bread. Washing his sandwich down with a glass of water, he bolted out the door within five minutes of his arrival.

Shortly before noon, I rose to answer a knock on the door. A deliveryman stood on the porch holding a long, narrow box marked, "HOSPITAL GUARD RAILS."

Closing the door behind me, I hung my head in abject sorrow at the bitter irony. We received these rails ... the last remaining item needed before we could bring Kim home ... on the very day I knew for certain she would go home ... but not to our residence on Walter Street. Wetting and smearing the ink, my tears plop-plopped upon the cardboard box. Nothing could obliterate the pain.

Still aching with the same strange exhaustion, I crawled back into the bed. This was the first time in weeks I had been away from Kim for any length of time. I wanted so badly to return to her, but I had no vehicle at home, and my legs couldn't bear my weight to walk the ten-block distance. Later, I realized this was God's way of giving Dan the remaining time with Kim.

Seeing his little girl in such agony caused him visceral pain. If given the choice, instead of sitting in a hospital room, he would have preferred to find doors to batter down, or towers to topple, if either might somehow protect our child from the ravages of this excruciating disease. Yet on this last day, he stood in as her caregiver because of my need for rest. I understood his feelings of absolute helplessness in the midst of such torment, but I am certain it comforts him today when he remembers those last hours he spent alone with Kim.

I give unending praise to God for his overall planning in

our lives. His perfect orchestration of each day and each hour left no room for lingering regrets in our hearts. We have pain and sorrow, but we have no regrets. While on earth, Kim knew nothing but love. While sick, we gave her our devotion and the best medical care possible. In death, we stood beside her. Dan alone shared this last day with her—to stand as her protector, and to nurture the special bond of love existing between a daddy and his little girl.

In the early part of the afternoon, the hospital staff informed Dan, "Your child's life is ebbing. It's time to alert the family and bring your wife to the hospital."

I expected it. When I heard the front door open, I knew the reason for Dan's return. He spoke calmly and quietly. "Kim's breathing is slow and labored. This might not mean anything at all—just like the other night—but the nurses thought I should come and get you."

I nodded in agreement; we were both avoiding the truth. This time we did not expect a reprieve from the hands of death. I dressed quickly and rode with Dan to the hospital while prevailing upon God for another favor. "Please Lord, grant me one last thing. Let us be with her when she meets you. Please don't take her until we get there!"

We met nurses inside the hospital who attempted to reassure us, but once we drew near to Kim, any false hope quickly evaporated. Death blanketed her face as she struggled and fought for every breath. Her legs and feet were blue with cold, and I searched for a blanket to warm her before sending friends for my parents.

Mother arrived shortly thereafter, but my Dad, with a newly broken ankle, could not be reached and transported in time. Friends and nurses filled the room while Mother, Dan, and I spoke our last words to Kim.

I wanted so much to hold my Kimmie as Jesus came for her, but she would not be able to catch another breath if my arms held her one last time. I could only lower my body over hers and kiss her sweet face. "I love you precious baby. I love you Kimmie Dawn! Remember, I will see you soon. I will hear your voice, and come running."

Dan gently kissed her hand while clutching it tightly over his heart. Mother stood at the foot of the bed touching and warming Kim's legs, while softly cooing words of love. Then with one last breath, and one deep grimace, Kimmie took her flight. The room trembled in silence.

Dan looked across the bed. His eyes seared into mine. "Is she gone, Mom?"

"Yes," I replied. "Yes, honey; she's gone."

> *In the heavens above, and in the earth below, a Holy God exists who sees every sorrow and heartache. He collects a mother's tears, and gathers her child into his arms to offer comfort—until one bright day when the mother and child are reunited in Glory.*

CHAPTER 40 - VICTORY LAP IN HEAVEN

Kimmie left us on Wednesday, the fifteenth day of May, at three-thirty in the afternoon ... exactly three months from the date she was first hospitalized. The moments and hours following her death are only hazy memories. I remember silently thanking God for his mercy, and I remember the kindness of Dr. Paul and friends. I also remember Dan and I leaving the hospital as soon as possible to inform Dirk of his sister's passing. We didn't want our son to hear the news from anyone else. We needed to deliver this message in person.

As we stepped out of the room, we witnessed a nurse in the hallway weeping for our daughter. For once, tears did not fall from my eyes. I felt only a great sense of relief, coupled with thankfulness to God, for taking Kim from her suffering.

Just as we were exiting the doors of the hospital, we met my Dad who was whispering the words, "Blessed Heavenly Father," while tears welled in his eyes. We had no need for words; he knew Kim's struggle had ended.

We drove to Mother and Dad's business where our son waited with Ben. Dan lifted Dirk into his arms. "Son, Mom and I thought we'd take you home with us so we can spend some time together."

Wise beyond his years, Dirk sat between us on the ride home never uttering one word. Our faces portrayed the truth in vivid detail. Offering small talk to break the silence, we ushered him into our home and sat down on the couch. Refusing to sit with us, our son stood at attention. O Lord, how do we make this reality easier for him?

I attempted to gather Dirk into my arms, but he pulled backward, and stared into my eyes.

"Did Kim go to heaven?" he demanded.

Dan and I simultaneously gasped.

Choking back a sob, I answered. "Yes honey; she went to heaven."

Dirk wiped tears from his eyes while he bravely stated, "Well, I bet Kim can run faster than me now."

Yes, I thought; it's amazing. Kim is now completely healed; never again will she suffer pain or tears. I thanked God for his love. I thanked him also for our wonderful son who at last sought comfort in my arms. At six years of age, with his life now dramatically altered, Dirk understood one important thing: Kim's life did not end with her earthly death. He envisioned his sister running in heaven, free at last from her imprisonment within a motionless body. The words of a child once again spoke directly to the heart of the situation.

Death stealthily came like a thief, and robbed us of the presence of our beautiful child, but death did not win. Jesus, along with thousands of angels, escorted her to the arms of God. Death won a momentary victory, but the ultimate, lasting victory belonged to Kim through Jesus Christ.

> *"But they that wait upon the Lord shall renew their strength; they shall mount up with wings as eagles; they shall run, and not be weary; and they shall walk, and not faint" (Isa. 40:31).*

CHAPTER 41 - ALIVE WITH JESUS

Our home echoed with emptiness. Nothing seemed real. Our departure from the hospital was very different from the one I envisioned for so many months. I dreamed of Kim holding my hand and walking down the steps of the hospital while she waved goodbye to her beloved nurses. Instead, Dan and I walked away holding on to one another for strength. Never again would there be a little blue-eyed Kimmie Dawn walking between us, and lifting her feet so we could swing her back and forth. Her absence from our home screamed at us while Dirk, attempting to act much older than his years, sat in silence.

Near the door still lay the package marked, "GUARD RAILS." Its presence mocked and taunted us. I randomly drifted throughout our home. In every room, I found a silent reminder of what was once ours. I spied the booster seat still poised in her chair at the table, Kim's new coat hanging in the closet, and misplaced shoes under the bed. A tattered and well-loved doll sat in the wooden rocking chair—waiting for her little girl to return.

I pulled up a corner of Kim's coverlet, and brought it to my cheek. Inhaling a whiff of a lingering scent, I wondered how long I could treasure her sweet fragrance.

Tears fell when I stepped into the room we had prepared for Kim's homecoming, but I would not, and could not wish her back. Kim received the ultimate healing ... exceeding that of any earthly physician ... and she was happy because she was with Jesus.

Word of Kim's death spread rapidly. Dear friends and family members flooded our home. Our church family, along with perfect strangers, brought gifts of food and flowers. Dan and I sensed it was more difficult for them than it was for us. They lamely searched for words, but none came. We understood; true words of comfort did not exist, but then, none were really necessary. Our God richly provided us with all the comfort we needed. His Spirit would give us strength and peace over the ensuing days.

Hours later, after the last visitor exited our home, I lay in bed trembling. Dan, thinking I was crying, sought to comfort me. "Honey," he began, as he tightened his arms around me, "it's all right; you know she's with God. Nothing will ever hurt her again."

I squeezed his hand. "That's not the reason for my trembling. I was thinking about the amazing power of God we just witnessed. For three months we have prayed for God's will to be accomplished. There were times when the answer seemed so slow in coming I didn't know whether I should expect an answer. Then, just because we kept holding on, Jesus came. In the twinkling of an eye, he answered our plea for mercy. God didn't deny one single thing we asked of him.

"Last night when Cliff and I walked back from the chapel, I sensed the presence of death the moment I entered Kim's room. I knew God would take her soon. Maybe that's why I couldn't stay there today. But honey, I've never fully experienced God's power in the way I did today. I have never seen it work in such a marvelous way, nor so quickly, just because we asked it of him."

Yet my faith is so small. By five o'clock in the morning, I

began to have doubts. "Lord, I don't know if I can bear to see Kimmie dead ... in a casket. I don't think I can do it!"

I wanted to run away again. I longed to escape what lay ahead, but somehow, in order to honor my brave daughter, I must do the unthinkable. By mid-morning we received the call from the funeral home, and the queasiness erupted. Nausea gripped my body. O God, give me strength!

I squeezed Dan's hand tightly as we walked up to the white, velvet-covered casket. Flowers filled the room; a cloyingly sweet scent permeated the air. My stomach rebelled. Nausea bubbled up once more. Wretched sickness constricted my throat when we approached the bier, but Dan held my hand firmly in his. "We'll get through this together," he reminded.

I closed my eyes for a brief moment to fortify myself, then peered into the casket. Instantly, the fear and sickness vanished. I looked down upon a stunning little girl lying peacefully still. The child wore the beautiful pink gown and robe Mary gave Kim on her birthday. A sparkling aquamarine ring encircled the child's third finger of her left hand, but this was not our little girl. The child's features ... a tiny nose, cupid's mouth, and long eyelashes ... resembled those of Kim's, but this was not our Kimmie.

Dan and I turned toward one another in awe and with relief pouring over our souls. The Holy Spirit simultaneously revealed to us a powerful truth in this viewing: Kimmie's not dead! She is alive! DEATH IS ONLY THE BEGINNING OF ETERNAL LIFE.

We accepted the biblical teaching of life after death. In fact, our faith in this sustained us throughout our entire ordeal, but not until this very moment did we fully comprehend its meaning. The instant we saw her, we understood the essence we loved and cherished about Kim had never been her beautiful body ... but something inexplicable and very real ... existing *within* her body.

We loved her spirit, and now it was gone. Kim's essence was not dead within a lifeless shell, but rather, somehow miraculously gone! When Kim's spirit fled that frail and diseased frame, her body changed so much we hardly recognized this as our daughter. We had no need to *hope* Kim was with God; we saw the irrefutable proof. She was alive and living with God! In this moment of revelation, God's greatest comfort came into our hearts when we realized with certainty we would see our Kimmie again.

After a long and trying day, night mercifully fell. The solitude of darkness allowed me to meditate upon God's love before succumbing to the exhaustion overwhelming me. Yet, I did not fall into an ordinary sleep. As thoughts and events filtered through my mind, Kim appeared to me in a vision. Clothed in white; her hair was once again long and blond, and she was cradled in someone's arms.

At first, I saw only my beloved child, but then the focus became clearer. Although I never glimpsed a face other than hers, I noticed the hands of the one who held my daughter so lovingly. They bore the imprint of nail scars. He wore white raiment, and he and Kim were seated on a chair much like a throne. Those scarred hands drew Kimmie nearer to him. In the distance, I heard the faint echo of a "Love Story" forever etched upon my heart.

"You know what, Mom? I love you, and I love Daddy. And I love Dirkie ..."

Her delicately sweet voice receded. Kim looked upward into the eyes of the one who held her.

"And you know what, Mom? I love Jesus. And Jesus loves me."

Kim pivoted her gaze from the one who held her and looked toward me. "Mom, I love you. My head don't hurt no more."

As Kimmie slowly faded from my sight, the following words echoed in the distance: "Everything is all right."

Dan and I said goodbye to our daughter in the crowded sanctuary of the small church we attended. The room was filled to capacity with those who came to morn with us. Flowers festooned both sides of the miniature white casket. One special arrangement of pink roses displayed a card signed with the names of Kim's beloved nurses. May added a short message: "Don't cry for Kim; she is with God, and God is love."

The pastor spoke of heaven and its glory while we looked at one another and smiled. Our Father's assurance that we would see Kim again rested upon us. We buried her frail body without tears, because we knew with all certainty that she was not inside the white velvet box. We rejoiced with Kim in her triumph over death. Just think of it; Kimmie has touched the face of Jesus! Heaven became a much sweeter place for us.

Road of Grace
There is a road that leads to heaven. Jesus lights the way.

A path where God's mercy is given. A road we call Grace.

Epilogue

The days since Kim's death have not been easy, but the pain lies only in her absence from our lives. One sweet voice is forever missing from the cacophony of family gatherings and activities. We continue to rejoice and praise God for his goodness and mercy. We thank him for giving us this very special child who led others to Christ though her suffering.

We still think of Kim as our miracle child. Some may ask, "She died; where is the miracle?"

Miracles come in all forms and sizes. Some enter our lives with fanfare. Others come so softly we'll miss their appearance ... until we search our hearts and see the transformation of our souls by God's hand.

The miracle appeared in our lives when we learned to depend upon God, fully and completely, to meet our needs. We learned we can do nothing separate and apart from Jesus Christ. We no longer dread death because an example has been set for us, and we know Kim awaits us with Christ in heaven.

What great peace I have received, knowing no matter what the world may throw at me, I have Jesus! The Savior lives inside of me. He goes before me into battle—knocking down doors I am too afraid to open—while he surrounds me with his peace. His blood has sealed our relationship both now and forever.

So many times during Kim's illness, I wanted to pick her up

and run to a place of safety. Only in the last days of Kim's life did I at last understand this was truly possible. I simply needed to pack up my fears and run straight into the arms of Jesus. He stood there all along, patiently waiting for me.

When we bare our souls before God, our heartaches are converted into a stronger and more intimate relationship with him. Our sorrows develop a complete trust between the Father and his child. No matter which tribulation we experience in our lives, we will never be alone. Jesus will walk ahead of us. He will shield us from the lurking dangers and offer his cloak of protection.

A woman visited me shortly after Kim's death. With perfect poise, she stated, "If you had more faith, your child would still be alive."

Is faith greater when God answers our pleas in the way we desire, or do we develop greater faith and trust when life strips us of all we hold dear?

I will leave the final judgement on this question to God. No one else can determine our degree of faith. But I am certain of this one thing: If we were perfect, we wouldn't need a Savior.

> *"For I am persuaded, that neither death, nor life, nor angels, nor principalities, nor powers, nor things present, nor things to come, nor height, nor depth, nor any other creature, shall be able to separate us from the love of God which is in Christ Jesus our Lord" (Rom. 8:38–39).*

The storm came upon us. It shook our foundation; it battered our souls and flooded our hearts, but Jesus stood in the midst to anchor us in his love. He led us through the valley of grief, and upheld us when we were too weak to stand.

Yes, God took our little Kim home, but he did not desert

us afterward. He visited us with his spirit to comfort and give us peace. He left us with a wonderful son, and another beautiful daughter who commanded her very own place in our hearts. Both have given us joy, and great pride in their accomplishments ... just as God intended.

When the voluminous amount of hospital and medical bills arrived, God's hand held us and provided for our needs abundantly. Friends established a medical fund for Kim, and hundreds within the community bounteously contributed.

We were astounded by Dr. Carlton's generosity as well. After month upon month of continuous medical care, visiting twice daily, and performing two surgeries, we were stunned when we received his bill. Only one charge was listed on the statement. The surgeon charged us for Kim's first surgery to implant the shunt. The rest of the page was blank.

The words, *"Everything is all right,"* echoed in my head long after Kim's death. At night, when the reality of my lengthy separation from Kim overtook me, I slipped from the bed and sought solace in the darkness. My Savior met me each time, and offered me comfort and shelter. While in his arms, I was free to become the wretched, grieving mother who yearned to see and touch her child once more. I cried without condemnation, and mourned openly because I was in the arms of my Safe Haven.

A few weeks following Kim's death, I traveled back to the hospital where Kim spent the last months of her life. For the final time, I climbed the stairway to the Pediatric Ward. I intended to personally thank each of Kim's former caregivers, but only two were available.

Liz informed me, "Most of the nurses who took care of Kim asked to be reassigned to other floors following her death."

Betty took me aside, "Timmy is back in the hospital. This time he won't be going home. He's entered the final stage of his battle with leukemia."

She took my hand, and led me toward his room while I searched for an excuse. "I ... , I don't know ... "

Betty gently prodded, "He needs you. He's all alone once again."

Trembling with fear, I reluctantly walked into a stark room devoid of toys, books, or a mother's touch.

I don't think I can do this! Oh Lord, not again!

Yet, the moment I neared his bed, Timmy riveted his huge, brown eyes upon me, and held out his arms for a hug.

"How is your little girl? Did she get all better?"

"Yes Timmy, she is all better. Her head doesn't hurt any more. She gets to run and play every day now. Honey, pretty soon you will be all better too. I love you Timmy. Jesus loves you too."

Timmy left this world just a few days later. When I read his name in the paper, I knew for certain he no longer lived alone and afraid. I like to think Kimmie welcomed him to heaven and introduced him to the angels. His death reminded me that this life is meant to be a journey—not our ultimate destination.

Following each shattering event in our lives, God reaches down from heaven with unfathomable love to patch us back together again, piece by piece, making us better than we were before.

Prayer

Heavenly Father, we thank you for your rich blessings. We thank you for answering prayers, not in our will, but in yours. We know your will for our lives is much better, and much greater than any of our own plans.

I thank you for breaking me down, for humbling me in my weakness, so you could remold me into the person you wanted me to become. Father, it is a daily struggle, and I continue to stumble and fall over my own pride. Thank you for never giving up on me—even when I fail so miserably.

Father, Dan and I are most especially thankful for our children—a son who demonstrates incredible strength of character, a daughter who has a generously loving heart, and Kim who died glorifying your name.

Lord, not one hair of Kim's precious head has been touched without your knowledge. You made plans for her before you created the earth. You orchestrated each of her days. Your hand rests upon her. What shall we fear?

We understand the children you place in our lives are not ours. Your claim to them began long before they were born, but we thank you for seeing fit to trust us with their lives. We are grateful for having the privilege of caring for Kim these three years. We will not ask you to take care of her, because we know she is in much better hands than ours.

Finally, dear Father, we thank you for your son, Jesus, who died so each of us may one day enjoy the rich blessings you have prepared for us. We await thy return.
Amen.